Wilden, All Saints is a surprise! Situated in north Worcestershire on the outskirts of Stourport-on-Severn, the church's plain brick façade gives no clue as to the treasures within.

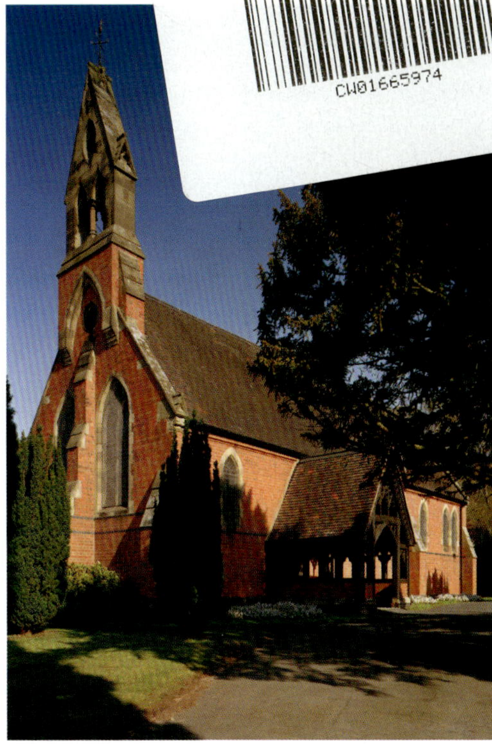

All Saints, Wilden. W.F. Hopkins, architect

Wilden's early history

The River Stour at Wilden has been the scene of industrial activity since the 16th century. In 1511 a fuller's mill was owned by William Baylly and by 1633 two corn mills were added, with the original mill converted into a slitting mill. The site was purchased by Richard Foley and passed to his son, Thomas, who added two forges. More industrial works were situated along the 24 mile stretch of the Stour than on any other river in England. By 1669 the word *ironworks* justifiably described the expanding site. The completion of the Staffordshire and Worcestershire Canal in 1768 was significant; the waterway was channelled close to Wilden before its junction with the River Severn. Three years later, the Wilden ironworks were leased to Thomas Hill and partners. A pattern emerged of buying and selling the land, each new owner extending the building and adding improvements. In 1830 one owner, W.T. Lewty, added steam power and a beam engine, then renamed it *The Wilden Iron and Tin Plate Company*. In 1835 a wharf built by Isaac Pratt enabled a link from the works to the canal network and major markets, but despite innovations, the works again changed hands due to bankruptcy. In 1840 the company was bought by the Baldwin family, headed by George Pearce Baldwin.

The Baldwin family

The Baldwins, a family of ironworkers, originated in Shropshire and already owned several local enterprises including an Iron Foundry and ***The Anglo American Tin Stamping Company,*** both in Stourport. Within months of acquiring the Wilden Ironworks George Pearce Baldwin died of scarlet fever and the company was left in the hands of his brother, Enoch, and George's sons, Pearce and William. The company began trading as *EP&W Baldwin of Wilden*. G.P. Baldwin's untimely death meant he never met his 12th child, Alfred, born in the spring of 1841.

Alfred was brought up by his mother, Sarah, daughter of a Methodist minister. When old enough, like all the Baldwin boys, Alfred joined the family firm, and by 1863 was in joint control of the

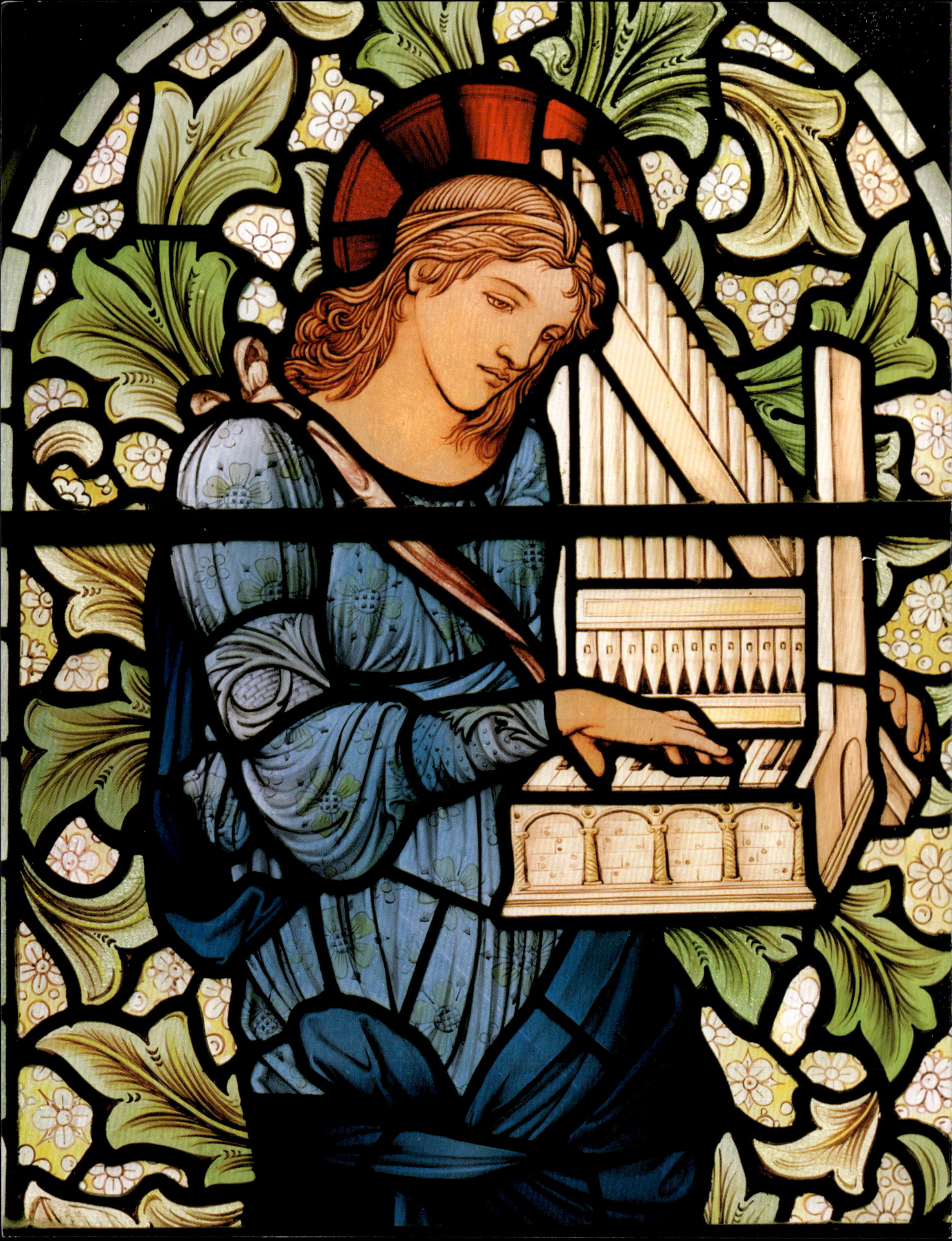

Wilden Works with his brothers George and Stanley. Alfred and his elder brothers followed the Methodist traditions of their Baldwin ancestors. They established a friendship with another family of Methodists, the MacDonalds. The two families met often in London where Reverend George Browne MacDonald had his ministry, and in return the MacDonalds would holiday in Stourport with the Baldwins. In 1864 during her stay in Stourport, Louisa, the minister's daughter, met Alfred. Louisa and Alfred became engaged in October 1865, marrying in 1866. This was a double wedding in St. Peter's Collegiate church, Wolverhampton as Louisa's sister also married. The significance of this marriage is evident later in the text.

Alfred and Louisa set up home in Lower Park, Bewdley. One year later, on 3rd August 1867, Alfred left for work at Wilden Ironworks, unaware that their child's birth was imminent. By the time he arrived home, Louisa had given birth to their only child, a son named Stanley. The servants are said to have carried the baby to the highest point in the house as a sign that he would *rise in the world.* This prophecy was duly fulfilled. In 1888, 21 year old Stanley joined the company as a partner, remaining in the business for 20 years before entering politics, ultimately becoming Prime Minister in 1923, 1924-29 and 1935-37.

Meanwhile Wilden works came close to bankruptcy through mismanagement by Alfred's brothers. In September 1870 aged 29, Alfred used loans from business associates to settle all debts, then bought out his brothers and took control. His acumen and hard work put the company back into profit. Alfred changed the company name to ***Baldwins Ltd*** and with his wife and child moved from Bewdley to Wilden. Wilden House lay across the lane from the forge and Alfred described the proximity of his home as *living over the shop.* When the west wind blew, smoke drifted into the house, but Alfred stated *dirt was acceptable along with the fortune it carried.* Alfred was a caring employer, a father-figure and benefactor who provided permanent employment and nearby accommodation for most of his workforce.

A church for Wilden

Alfred believed his duty of care extended beyond the factory floor, so when church commissioners agreed to provide the site for a church and land for burial, Alfred offered to erect a suitable church. In creating a parish for Wilden, a case had to be made to annex the parish from Hartlebury to the parish of Lower Mitton; the area being referred to as *Wilden Corner.* Much discussion ensued then on 10th July 1877 the Bishop of Worcester forwarded the plan to the Archbishop of Canterbury, Alfred's letter of 26th October 1877 followed, expressing his desire to build a church. Alfred gained permission, and on May 3rd 1879, laid the foundation stone for All Saints, Wilden.

Built by J. Cook of Hartlebury and designed by the Worcester Diocesan Architect, W.F. Hopkins, the church is described by Pevsner as *brick built with lancet windows.* Alfred stood the total cost of £3,000 including *fittings of stained pitch pine, an organ, boundary wall and other requisites.*

Left: St. Cecilia, detail

The original windows were of plain glass. In his diary, Alfred Baldwin recalls that on the 30th April 1880 he was hoping that all would be ready. On Sunday 4th May, 1880 Alfred met Bishop Philpott at the church at 11am and the service proceeded. Mr Haviland read the 1st Lesson, Mr Boyle the 2nd and the Bishop preached and conducted Holy Communion. There were 49 communicants, and the service lasted until 2pm. At 7.30pm the church was packed for Evensong, with *good offertories.* At the end of the day Alfred Baldwin records in his diary, *To bed, very tired, the work is done, thanks be to God, and may His blessings be on me and mine, and the whole Church.* Two years later, Alfred built the school, once again funding the project. Alfred and family were readily involved in all aspects of village life; church wardens, Sunday school teachers, school managers, hosts and benefactors.

Important marriages

Mundane expectations of this church, financed by a politician and built in an industrial hotspot are unfounded, for the church is blessed with an abundance of Arts and Crafts treasures. The explanation for this bounty lies in the family connections made through Alfred's wedding to Louisa on the same day as her sister's nuptials. Louisa's sister, Agnes, was engaged to Edward Poynter; Edward was a classical Victorian artist, and held the prestigious post of President of the Royal Academy in 1896, when he was also knighted. The couple arranged to marry in St. Peter's Collegiate church, Wolverhampton. Alfred and Louisa were to wed later, but their marriage was brought forward due to her father's ill health, thus the double wedding.

Two more of Louisa's sisters made notable marriages. Alice married John Lockwood Kipling and their son Rudyard found fame as an author. Georgiana married the Pre-Raphaelite painter, Edward Burne-Jones in 1860, after meeting through Henry, Georgiana's brother. This meant that Alfred Baldwin and Edward Burne-Jones became brothers-in-law, and this family relationship was crucial in the selection of window designs in Wilden.

Burne-Jones

Edward Coley Burne-Jones was born in Birmingham in 1833. He attended Exeter College, Oxford, reading theology, intending to become a clergyman. Here he met fellow students William Morris and Henry MacDonald, both of whom had an impact on his life. His interest in theology waned as his passion for literature and book illustration grew. He left university without completing his degree and moved to London where he and Morris studied art. Legends, fairy tales, romantic and heroic narratives became his favoured subject matter. Edward became friends with members of the Pre-Raphaelite Brotherhood: Dante Gabriel Rossetti, John Everett Millais and William Holman Hunt. This movement flourished between 1849-1853. They had sought to recreate the simple forms, bright colours and attention to detail featured in painting before the Renaissance. A year after Edward's marriage the company Morris, Marshall, Faulkner & Co. was founded, operating from 8 Red Lion Square, London. Edward and Georgiana's first home was nearby in Great Russell Street and they were regular guests of William and Jane Morris at Red House, Bexley Heath, which Burne-Jones helped to decorate.

William Morris was later a founder of The Arts and Crafts Movement. Solid working-class values and skilled craftsmanship typified the style of his followers both in painting and fine arts, whilst raising the artistic profile of crafting in glass, wood, textiles and metal. Burne-Jones's first commissions for stained glass window cartoons came from Messrs. Powell of Whitefriars, in 1857. From 1861 he designed exclusively for the firm of Morris, Marshall, Faulkner & Co. In 1881 the Company moved to Merton Abbey, the site of an ex monastery. It consisted of a house, workshops with out-buildings and two large two-storey sheds on either side of the River Wandle. A mill house, mill pond, meadow, orchard and vegetable garden were within the grounds. Morris adapted buildings to include a meeting room and a drawing and design room which later held a glass-firing kiln. There was a dormitory for apprentice boys, and altogether Merton Abbey factory employed around 100 people, producing painted glass windows, tapestries and carpets.

The Art of Glass

In ***Glass, Painted or Stained*** published in 1890, Morris wrote: *This art of mosaic window-glass is especially an art of the middle ages; there is no essential difference between its processes as now carried on and those of the 12th century.* Glass was coloured throughout its thickness by introducing different chemicals during its liquid state, for instance, gold is used to make red and cobalt to make blue. Glass was rolled and colour density determined its thickness. Morris & Co. bought their glass from James Powell & Sons, as this Whitefriars firm had rediscovered the technique through experimentation with medieval glass. Detailed lines of draperies and facial features were painted on using coloured opaque enamel. The enamel became part of the glass after being heated to 2000 degrees in a furnace. Sometimes glass would be fired twice to intensify colour but this added to the expense. Finally pieces of glass were fitted together with H-profile strips of lead and joints were soldered. Lead alone was not strong enough to support the weight of a window, so bars were used to reinforce it. These methods were virtually unchanged since medieval times, but the subject matter was now adapted to 19th century requirements. No longer did white-faced figures stand beneath ornate canopies, but characters had flesh-coloured faces and posed before rural backgrounds. Burne-Jones focused on figure design, while Morris determined colours, chose glass, designed background patterns, and arranged lead-work. Burne-Jones produced a cartoon, a full sized sketch, for each window commissioned. Cartoons were mainly black and white, and Burne-Jones would frequently comment that a typical charge of £200 for a large-scale window meant he was being grotesquely underpaid receiving £12 per cartoon. Extracts from Burne-Jones's account books reveal his complaints as cited by Schoenherr: *that his recent designs of St. Michael, St. George, Peace and Justice* are to be used for a *window in Berlin; that his payments for these, for two cartoons for the windows of St. Phillip's church, Birmingham, for Christ Blessing Children in Naworth, Cumberland, for Visiting The Sick and for Christ Entering Jerusalem for Marshall and Snellgrove, are inadequate, and accordingly his charges will henceforth be in guineas.*

Leading and glass painting processes were left almost entirely to interpretation by craftsmen supervised by Morris. Burne-Jones would occasionally leave comments on the work of studio artists, e.g. *Note from BJ- Is pleased with the Hawarden window; one of the topmost angels is over-shaded; feels that the musical instruments should be a subtle purply-brown colour with the near nimbuses in the same shade but paler.* Glass artists painted details of hair, facial features, and folds in drapery. Sewter lists more than 40 glass artists, some of these prominent in the production of Wilden's windows: William Stokes, for example, was a glass-painter who worked for Morris & Co. between 1880 and 1915. Thomas Bowman, probably the company's longest-serving employee, ranked amongst its best glass painters. George Titcomb, a glass stainer, moved from north London to be closer to Merton Abbey as did William Stokes. Christopher Baker Wren's father had also been a glass painter; Wren is listed in the 1881 census as a *glass painter and tobacconist* and 10 years later as a *glass painter and china dealer.*

Burne-Jones's cartoons of biblical scenes, saints and angels were compiled into a catalogue. Following the deaths of Morris in 1896 and Burne-Jones in 1898, Dearle took on the role of Artistic Head and Manager, and the firm continued to produce designs, referencing the catalogue and faithfully reproducing each line of chosen cartoons with great interpretation and technical skill. Dearle identified closely with the craftsmanship of Morris and artistry of Burne-Jones, and under his supervision the workshop productions rarely deviated from their stylistic ethos.

Wilden's Windows

In Medieval times, pictorial church windows were termed *A Poor Man's Bible.* Saints, angels and biblical scenes reminded mainly illiterate congregations of the prospect of heavenly afterlife earned by earthly commitment to faith. The original windows in Wilden church were plain glass, but between 1900 and 1914 these were replaced by the Morris & Co. windows, featuring Burne-Jones designs. Alfred Baldwin, mindful of the spiritual needs of his employees, chose many of these designs to support them in their journey of faith. Though Edward Burne-Jones had died in 1898, as brother-in-law to Alfred and Louisa it was appropriate that his designs were chosen. Church records list dates of placement, name the studio artists who worked on each window, and list the 'BJ' catalogue number which enables identification of the cartoon's original use, the frequency of use and location. Under Dearle Morris & Co. retained the 'BJ' catalogue and his designs were still available. Cormack notes these reappearances enhanced rather than detracted from their value. *New colourings, new backgrounds, new architectural settings mean that these figures, though arrestingly familiar, are actually never quite the same. Morris & Co windows have become part of the fabric of the nation, the absolute high point of Victorian church art.*

All Saints has 14 window spaces all of which are fitted with a Burne-Jones window. Other churches in Britain possess multiple Burne-Jones windows (for example St. Martin's, Brampton in Cumbria) however, Wilden is unusually blessed with its set of exclusively Burne-Jones/Morris & Co. windows, with perhaps only All Hallows, Liverpool being similarly distinguished. A clockwise tour of the church windows is described below, the Burne-Jones catalogue numbers appearing in brackets.

Right: The Minstrel Angel, detail

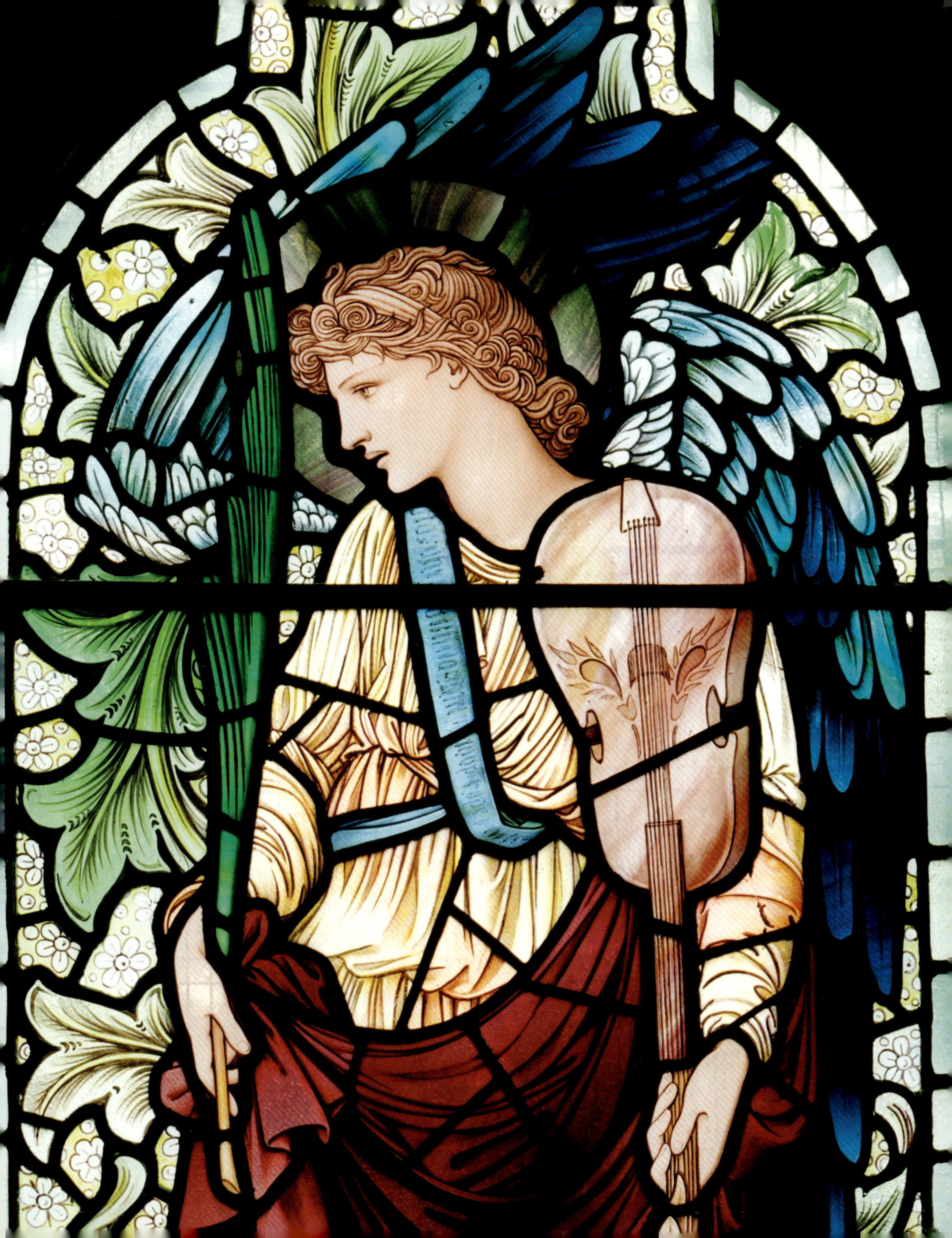

The East Window

One of the first windows to be replaced with a Burne-Jones design was the east window above the altar; a composite window divided into three tracery sections, three main panels in a middle tier and three smaller lower tier panels. It appears in Wilden's church records on 16/10/1902 and was gifted by Alfred and Louisa in recognition of their happy married life. The three tracery minstrel angels were painted by Wilson. At the apex is an ***Angel blowing double pipes*** (BJ 185). The lines of the two pipes as they point downwards draw the viewer's eyes to the figures below, where offset left and right are two blue-winged ***Angels with dulcimers***, (BJ 430 & 431), originally designed for Holy Trinity church, Sloane Street, also used in St. Mary's church, Oxted. In the middle row large panels depict St. Martin, Christ Blessing the Children and St. George, from left to right viewed from the nave.

St. Martin, or ***Generosity*** (BJ 398), was painted by Stokes and originally designed for the east window at Brampton, in 1880. The legend of St. Martin tells how a Roman soldier riding with troops came across a near-naked beggar at the roadside. Pitying him, he divided his cloak and gave him half the garment. Later Christ came to St. Martin in a dream revealing that he himself was that beggar. Martin had been tested, but proved his good character and his conversion to Christianity followed. Burne-Jones made numerous pencil sketches in notebooks and this figure illustrates his skilled interpretation of draperies and fascination with armour. The representation of St. Martin does not focus on Roman military allegiance but is romantically heroic with winged helmet and soft drapes. The model's shapely calves are clad in red, but the brown, laced-up walking shoes seem an anomaly here. The alternative title of this figure, ***Generosity*** recalls the Arts and Crafts Movement's favoured subjects of virtues depicted as characters e.g. ***Humility*** and ***Patience.*** At Brampton, St. Martin or ***Generosity*** appeared in the sequence including ***Faith, Hope and Charity.***

The middle panel in this row depicts ***Christ Blessing The Children*** (BJ 45); painted by Watson, it shows Christ in red, and children in white and pink. In 1892, Burne-Jones had been commissioned to design a pair of stained glass windows for Hillhead church, Glasgow. Only one of those panels is replicated in the Wilden window, and the right hand panel showing mothers watching was not used. As the central panel it is still a very strong image. This design also appears in Oxted and both appear in the Burne-Jones window in SS. Peter & Paul, Wadhurst.

On the right in the middle tier is St. George or ***Courage*** (BJ 397), painted by Bowman. St. George is depicted in white armour, a blue tunic, another fanciful helmet and equipped

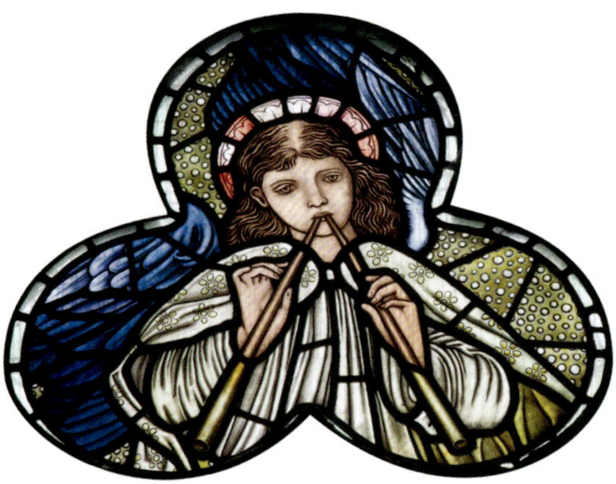

Angel blowing double pipes, east window detail

with a lance and red shield. Like St. Martin, this was originally designed for Brampton and commissioned by George Howard, 9th Earl of Carlisle. Howard's daughter gave these designs to Tullie House in Carlisle, an Art Gallery where they may still be viewed. Burne-Jones's account book of May 1880 describes the Brampton commission as *a colossal work of fifteen subjects - a masterpiece of style, a chef d'oevre of invention, a capo d'opera of conception - fifteen compartments - a herculean labour -hastily estimated in a moment of generous friendship for £200, - but it will remain equally a monument of art and ingratitude - £200.* To our knowledge there is no existing account of the cost of the Wilden windows, but we may assume Alfred paid considerably more than £200.

The lower panels comprise ***Reception into Paradise***, ***Adoration*** and ***Guardian Angel***. ***Reception into Paradise*** (BJ 618) was painted by Wilson. This was also first installed at Brampton in a circular window. Although in Wilden this is a small panel, it is the vital conclusion to Alfred's *Poor Man's Bible* message as it depicts faithful souls being received into heaven.

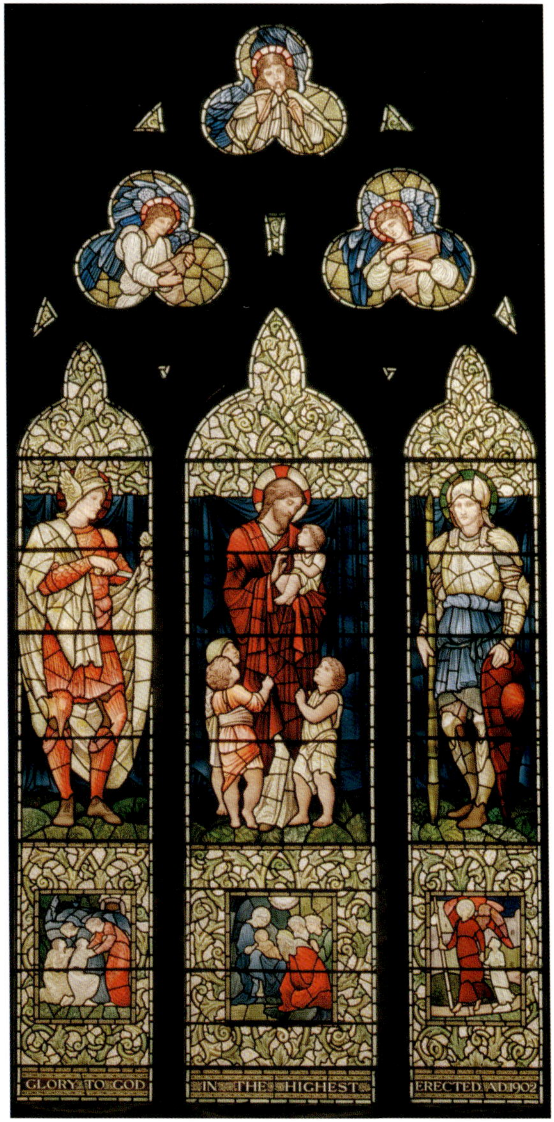

The east window

The Child with Guardian Angel (BJ 40) painted by Cory, is in the lower right panel. The angel is dressed in red, has pink and red wings and carries a staff on which is tied a bundle reminiscent of Dick Whittington seeking streets paved with gold. This was locally believed to show Stanley Baldwin setting out on life's journey led by his guardian angel, yet all of the Wilden windows postdate Burne-Jones, who died two years before the earliest was produced. The small figure is likely to be Margaret Burne-Jones, daughter of Edward and Georgiana. The design first appeared in Rottingdean church, where in 1893 three windows were installed in the chancel commemorating

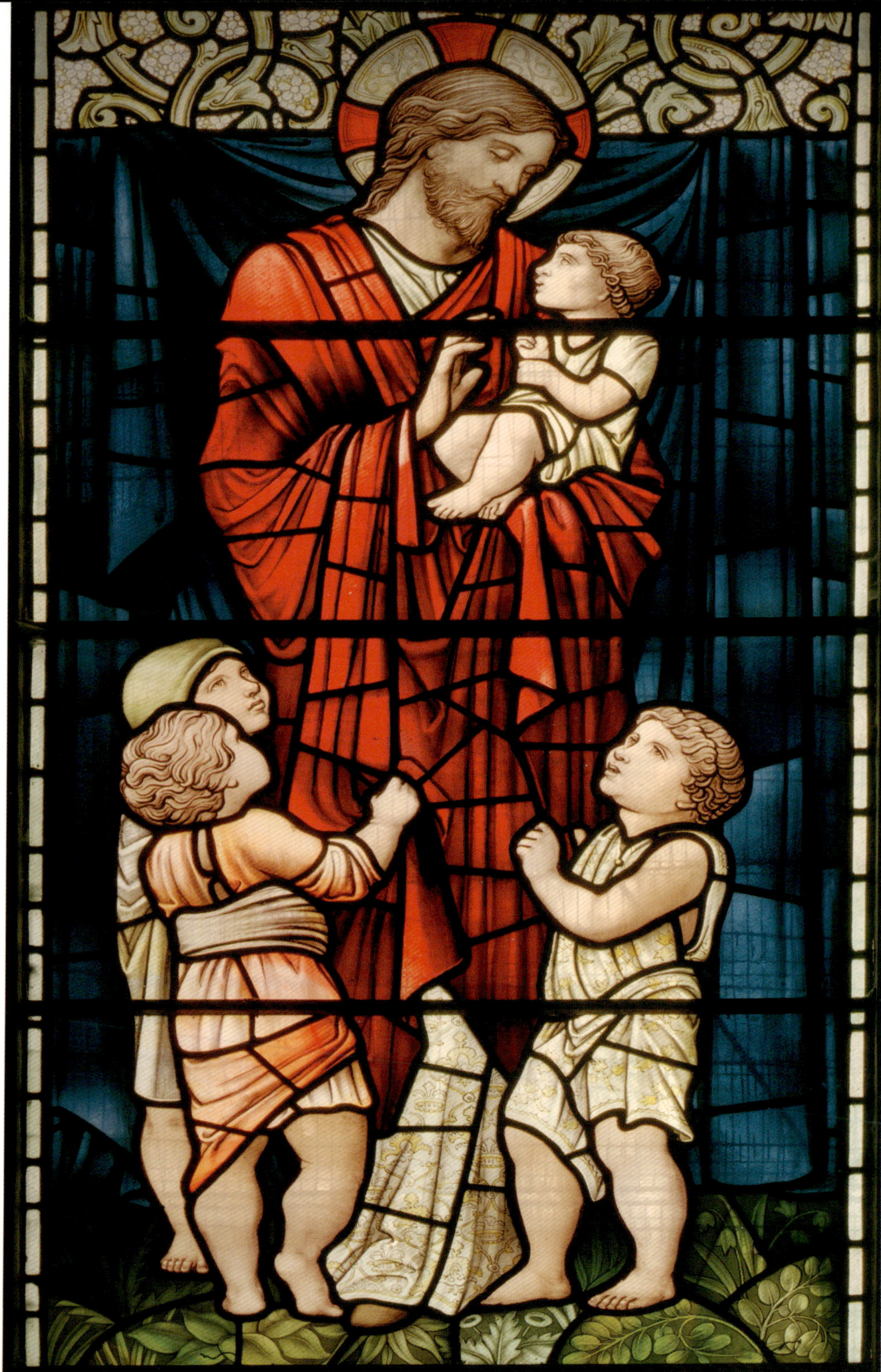

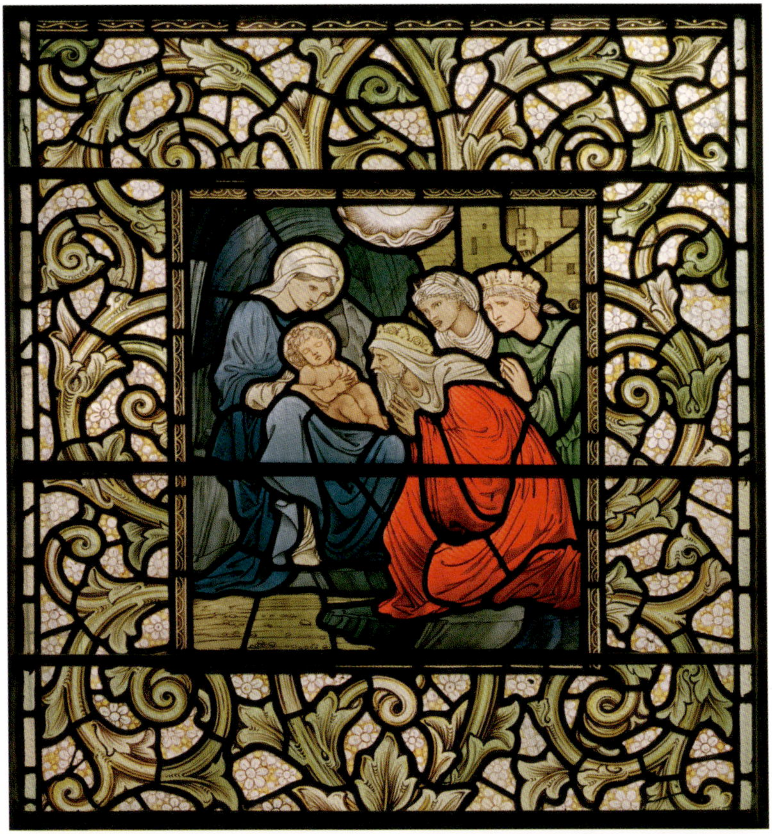

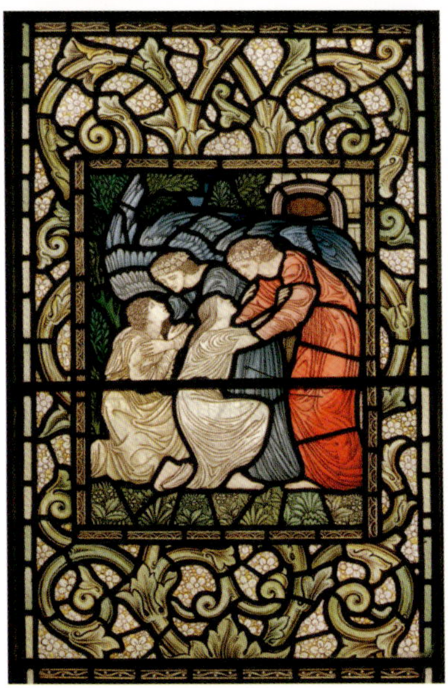

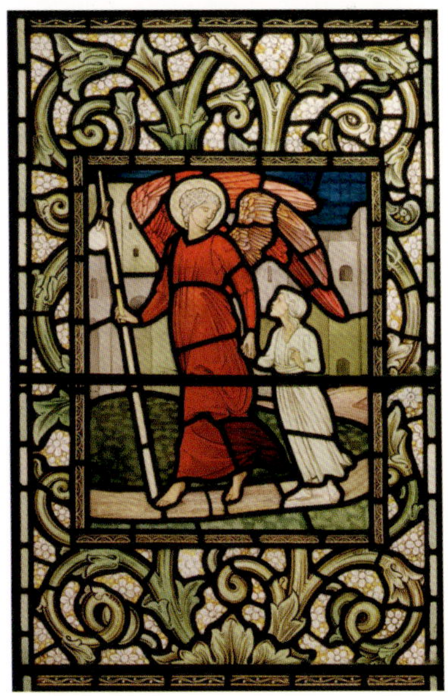

Previous pages: East window details: Christ Blessing the Children, The Adoration of the Magi, Reception into Paradise and The Child with Guardian Angel

Below: St. Martin

Right: Angel with dulcimer

Far Right: St. George

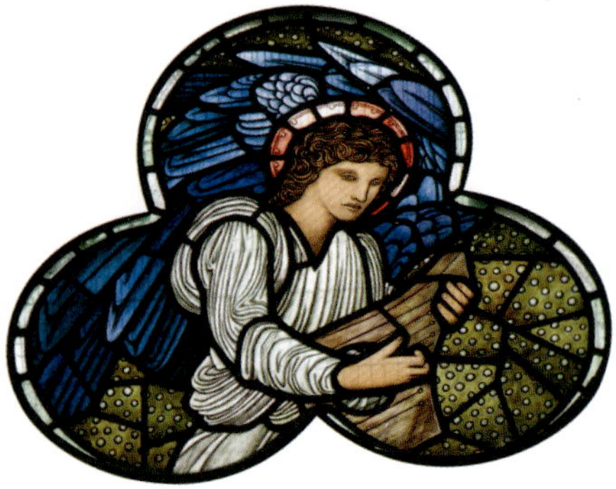

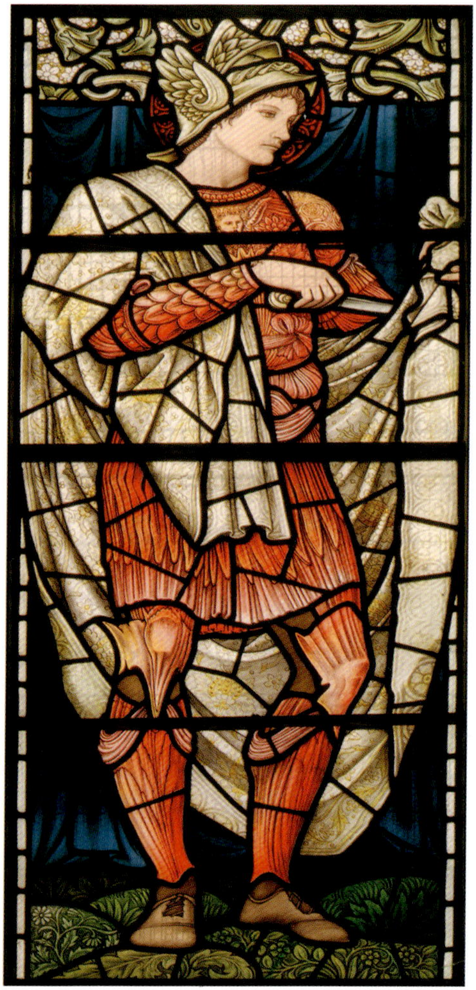

Margaret's marriage, including this design of Raphael, guardian of little children.

The Adoration of the Magi (BJ 305) was painted by Cory. Similar versions may be seen at Whitton, near Ludlow, and Boughton, Chester. The Magi kneel, gazing on the sleeping baby; two wear crowns while the third is black and wears a cloth turban. Across the base of the window, the inscription reads ***Glory to God in the Highest. Erected 1902.*** This composite window was viewed weekly by a congregation from Alfred's workforce and management committee. It is likely that these subjects were chosen in order to send out a message. Devoutly entrenched in his own beliefs, the pictorial elements reminded Alfred's workers of the difficulties encountered on the road to paradise. *The Adoration of the Magi* and central depiction of ***Christ Blessing the Children*** show the importance of treasured children at the heart of family life. Their innocence calls for spiritual guidance along life's way, and adulthood brings trials and dangers. While angels watch over all, saintly and allegorical role models lead faltering mortals towards paradise - a stern but well-intended lesson.

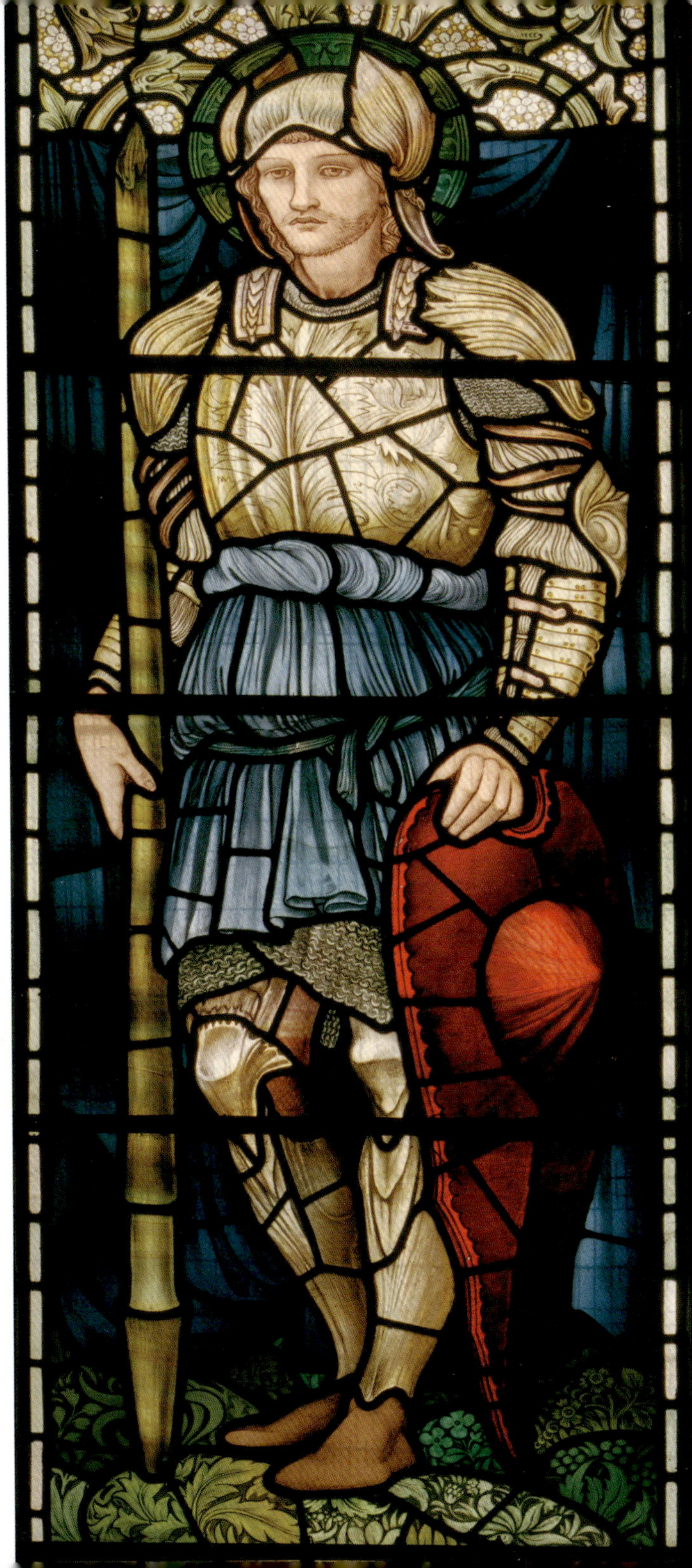

The Chancel Windows

In the chancel or choir area are three windows appropriately associated with music; ***St. Cecilia,*** a ***Minstrel Angel*** and ***Miriam.*** These windows appear in Wilden's records of 1902 and were donated by Roger Beck, a member of the Wilden Works Management Committee.

St. Cecilia (BJ 160), painted by Watson, wears a blue gown with extra drapes around her hips. St. Cecilia died a gruesome martyr's death in AD 230 after refusing to relinquish her faith, and as she lay dying she sang praises to God. She is the Patron Saint of Music, and is often depicted playing a hand organ, although she may be shown with harp, harpsichord, violin or flute. Here the accompanying inscription reads: ***Praise Him with the stringed instruments and organ*** (Psalm 150: 4). Burne-Jones's model for the image of Saint Cecilia was Mary Dahlgren Astor, wife of the financier William Waldorf Astor. Mary was well known in the 1890s in fashionable society on both sides of the Atlantic. Burne-Jones's first St. Cecilia cartoon was designed in 1867 for St. Saviour's Leeds and was also used in 1873 in Jesus College Chapel, Cambridge. The Wilden version is from the later design of 1874 produced for Christ Church Cathedral, Oxford, which has since been used in at least 27 instances.

The Minstrel Angel with palm and violin, (BJ 161), wears purple over pale yellow and has blue wings. The figure was painted by Titcomb, and like the other chancel figures appears against a William Morris designed background of acanthus leaves. In Christianity the palm is symbolic of triumph and rejoicing, and is especially associated with Jesus's triumphal entry into Jerusalem, celebrated on Palm Sunday. The inscription reads ***Praise Him all ye angels of His.*** The Minstrel Angel design was also used in Ribbesford, St. Leonard's church, where the figure is paler than the Wilden window, the angel wearing white against a pale blue background. The Ribbesford window was commissioned jointly by Edward Burne-Jones and Alfred Baldwin in memory of their mother-in-law, Hannah MacDonald. Hannah, mother of the MacDonald sisters was grandmother to both Stanley Baldwin and Rudyard Kipling, and in her later years lived in Bewdley to be near to Louisa. She died in 1875 and is buried in Ribbesford churchyard.

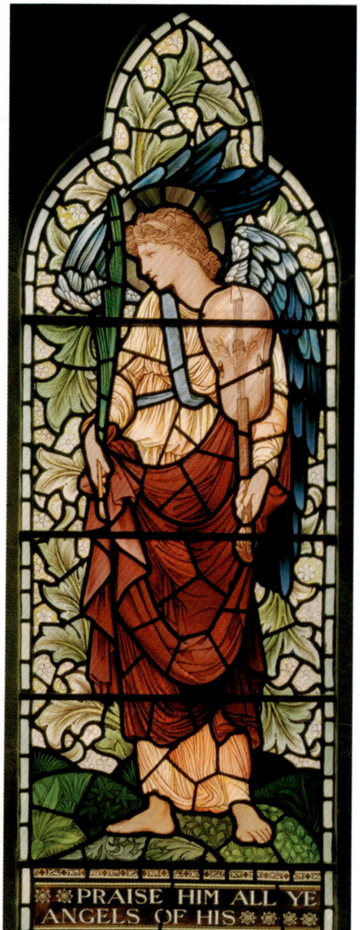

Right: The Minstrel Angel

Far Right: Miriam, detail

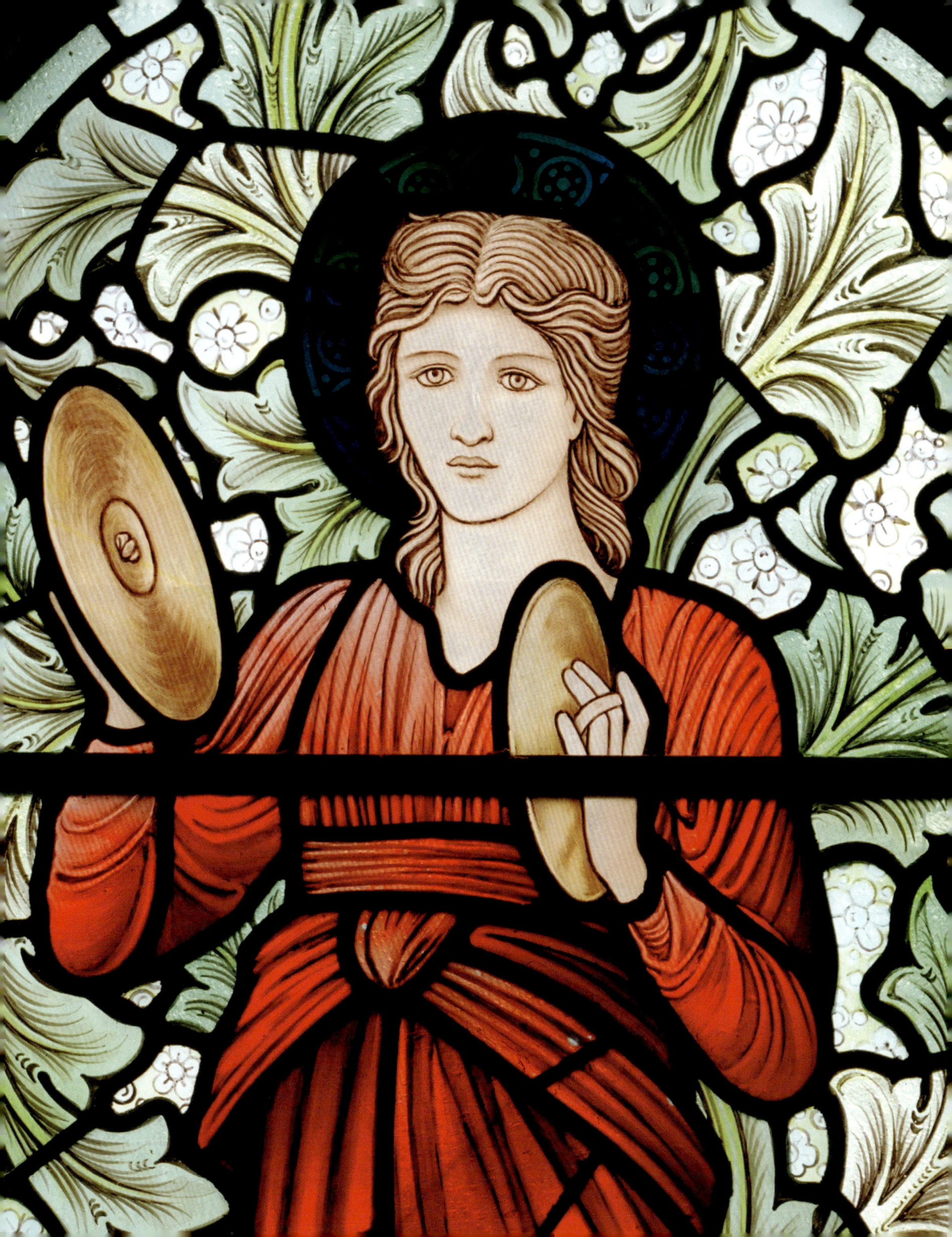

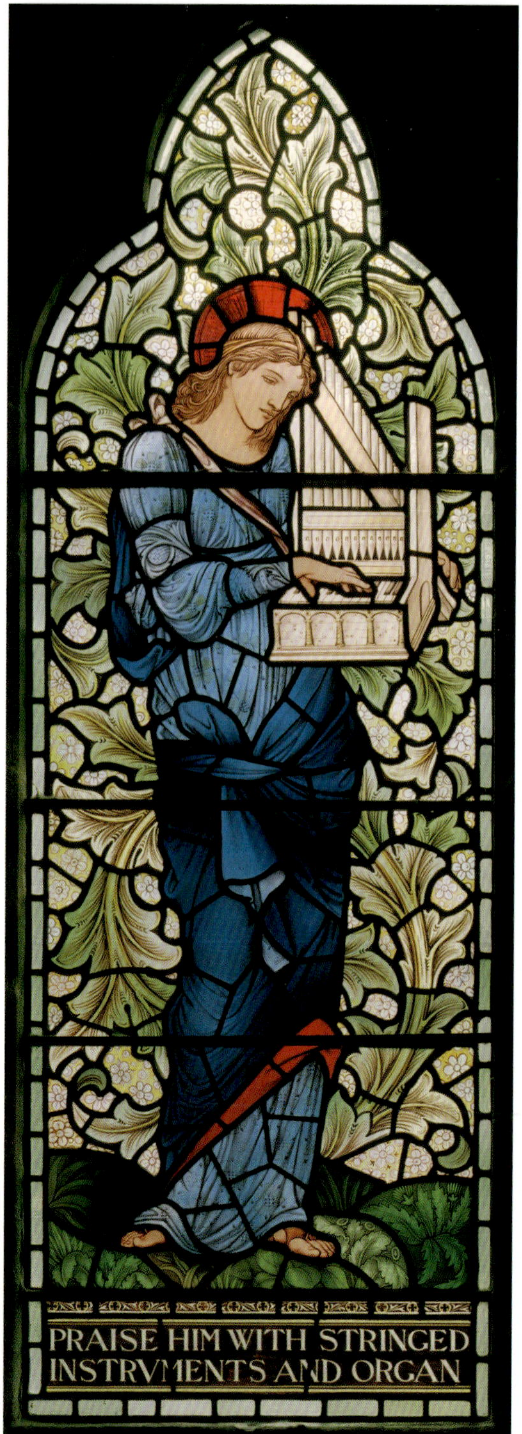
PRAISE HIM WITH STRINGED
INSTRVMENTS AND ORGAN

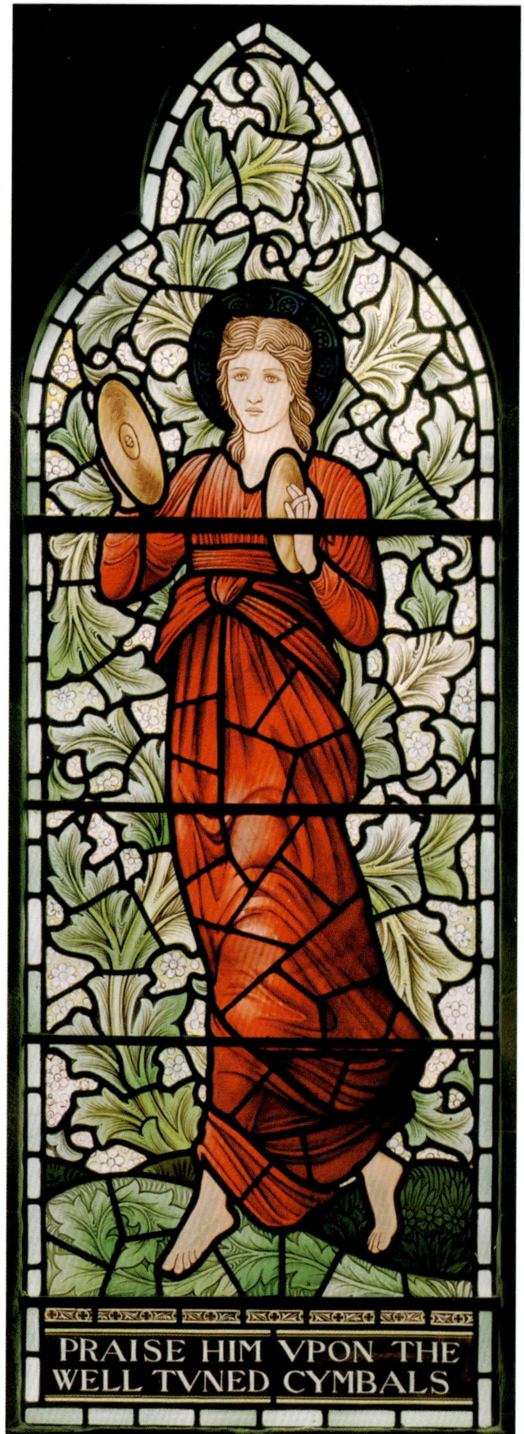
PRAISE HIM VPON THE
WELL TVNED CYMBALS

Miriam, (BJ 77), in red, was painted by Stokes, the background free-drawn by Knight, painted by Wren and the inscription ***Praise him upon the well-tuned cymbal***, was by Wren. Miriam was another subject Burne-Jones had drawn on earlier occasions. The version used here appeared for the first time in Ashton-under-Lyme in 1895 with the alternative title, ***Joy***. Miriam is best remembered for placing her baby brother, Moses, in the bulrushes. The adult Moses led the Israelites to the Promised Land, and after the passage through the parted Red Sea, Miriam sang a song of victory. According to Exodus when Pharaoh's horses, chariots and horsemen went into the sea, the Lord brought the waters of the sea back over them, but the Israelites walked through the sea on dry ground. Then Miriam the prophet, Aaron's sister, took a timbrel (or tamborine) in her hand, and all the women followed her, with timbrels and dancing. Miriam sang to them: *Sing to the Lord, for he is highly exalted. Both horse and driver he has hurled into the sea (15:20-21).* In this account she used a timbrel, but Burne-Jones shows her with cymbals.

Foliage and Joshua

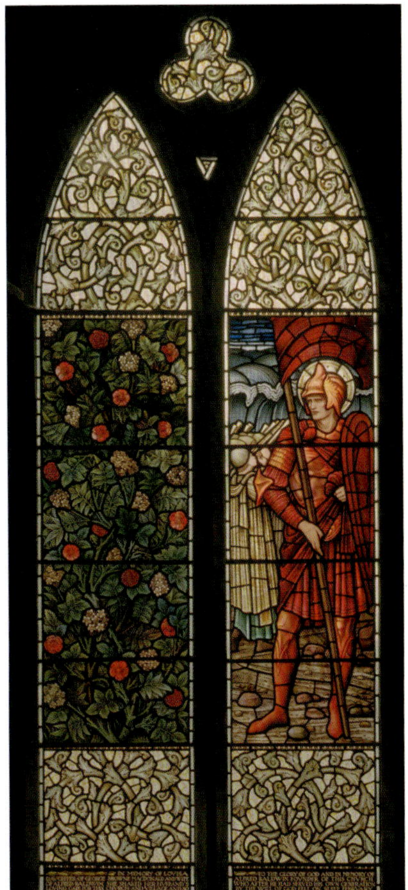

A two-light window was given by the directors of ***Baldwins Ltd*** in memory of their chairman, and installed a year after Alfred's death in 1908. Some 3,000 people attended his funeral. The window paid tribute to their beloved chairman who had also been their elected Member of Parliament, and Chairman of the Great Western Railway. From Alfred's modest introduction to the Baldwin Company he had risen to become a powerful industrialist and renowned politician, but his primary concerns remained his family and the Wilden workforce.

The rectangular panels known as ***Foliage and Joshua*** (BJ 471) were placed on 14/09/1909, with the Morris acanthus design filling spaces above and below. The Joshua panel is dedicated, ***To the glory of God and in memory of Alfred Baldwin, Founder of this church, who after he had served his generation by the will of God fell on sleep Feb. 13th 1908 aged 60 years.*** The Joshua figure wearing crimson was painted by Stokes and the background was drawn by Knight and painted by Watson. Church records state the grisaille heads and bases were drawn by Knight and painted by Watson. The subdued monochrome or 'grisaille' tones allowed the main figure to stand out. Crossing

Left: St. Cecilia and Miriam

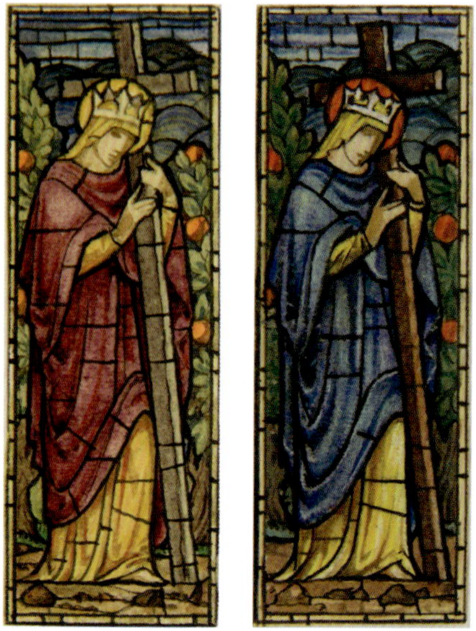

Lowndes & Drury sketches of St Margaret of Scotland, 1959. *The Worcestershire Archive and Archaelology Services*

the River Jordan was designed in 1885 for St. Giles's Cathedral, Edinburgh, where the scene extended over three panels. In Wilden only the central panel featuring Joshua and his trumpeters is used, and not the army of Israelites. Joshua is depicted in armour with spear and shield. In 1894, the actor Henry Irving commissioned Burne-Jones to design sets and costumes for a production of ***King Arthur.*** The play's cast starred Irving as Arthur and Ellen Terry as Guinevere. On viewing the costumes Burne-Jones commented, *The armour is good—they have taken pains with it.* In the Joshua figure Burne-Jones's fascination with armour is clear, there is detailed drawing, but it is theatrical and decorative rather than utilitarian.

Joshua was Moses's successor, and although Moses led the Israelites through the wilderness, it was Joshua who took command as they entered the Promised Land. *And when those who carried the ark came into the Jordan, the waters which were flowing down from above stood and rose up in one heap. So the people crossed opposite Jericho.* (Joshua 3:15-17). Jericho was the first city captured in Canaan as Joshua led the assault with his trumpeters. The name Joshua is a variant of Jesus, in English translating as ***Salvation***. This battle leader epitomised the longed-for Messiah. Significantly this figure was chosen for Alfred's panel as he himself had been a leader, championing the cause of workers and constantly aware of the moral fight against worldly evils. Burne-Jones provided the imagery for Alfred's window, but the inscription could never fully summarise his life and mission. Alfred's son later described how his father had talked of the *trumpet call* that inspired him in his life's work.

The memorial window was intended to commemorate Louisa's life too, though as Louisa was still alive, it was decided to install the foliage and roses filler panel until such time as she died. Louisa had requested the figure of St. Margaret of Scotland; Margaret, a queen, was wife to Malcolm III of Scotland and reputed to have had a good influence over her husband. Louisa had played a subservient, but companionably happy role in her marriage to Alfred, and in widowhood greatly missed him. The Morris floral design

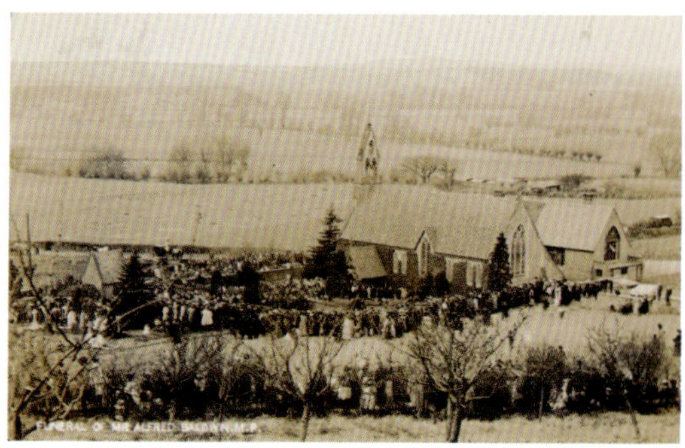

Alfred Baldwin's funeral. *The Ray Franks Collection*

has been used as a background to Burne-Jones's designs at Halewood, near Liverpool, and in Wilden, this vivid glass, though strikingly beautiful, has been a source of puzzlement as to why it remains. Louisa died in 1925, and over 30 years later the floral panel stood unaltered. The Worcestershire Archive and Archaeology Service holds fascinating correspondences between Earl Baldwin, Wilden PCC and Vicar, and a glass company, written between 1958 and 1960. The Earl, seeking to fulfil his grandmother's wishes, sought advice from a firm of Glassmakers, ***Lowndes & Drury,*** with a view to installing St. Margaret of Scotland. Mary Lowndes was active in the Arts and Crafts Movement, and in 1897 together with A.J. Drury, she founded ***Lowndes & Drury,*** based at The Glass House in Fulham. The company was thought capable of producing a sympathetic design, and claimed knowledge and access to all designs and records of the Morris firm. Although Morris & Co. had ceased production in the late 1930s, the design catalogue was largely available. The vicar arranged for a ladder and steps to be made available for *the window people* on the first visit of a representative who unfortunately was prevented from arriving by fog. A second visit was more successful and a bill of £24-12s-6d was duly submitted for journey expenses and preparing a coloured plan of the window. The cartoon produced showed St. Margaret wearing a purple robe. It was explained to the Earl that this hue was necessary to balance the vibrant red of Joshua. The Earl was unconvinced and requested the gown be blue. Changes were made, all seemed agreeable and plans were made to install St. Margaret next to Joshua and transfer the floral panel to the vestry. The cost of removing sections and supplying glass and craftsmanship would be £29-15s-6d. Preparing the vestry window to install the floral panel would cost £8-10s-0d. This was in 1959. At this point the Earl had misgivings as the glassmakers could not guarantee a perfect match with the Morris style. He decided not to proceed with pictorial elements, but to add a memorial inscription below.

This was not without its problems as there were several attempts to draft the tribute. One version acknowledged Louisa as a *writer of verse and prose,* another spoke of her 17 years of widowhood *remaining in Alfred's afterglow.* The vicar had the final say and the inscription reads: ***In memory of Louisa, daughter of George Browne MacDonald and wife of Alfred Baldwin. She shared her husband's loving care for this church and village and so continued until her death on May 16th 1925.*** The cost of inserting the memorial lines and fixing a brass plate to a pew was £3.3s.0d. In 1974 wire mesh window guards were renewed or added, costing £342.30.

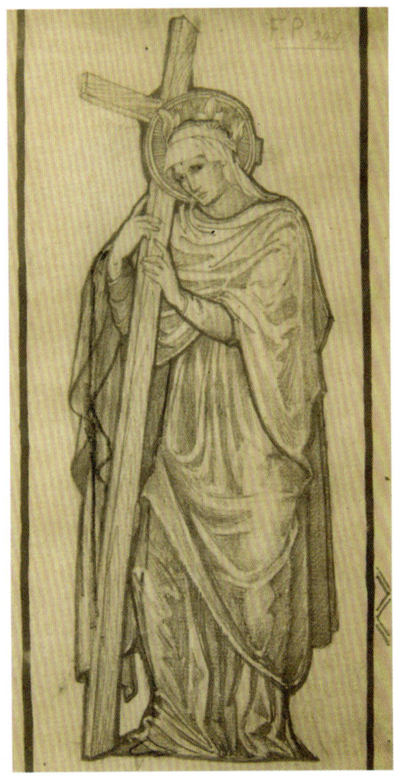

St. Margaret of Scotland. Morris & Co. pencil sketch after Burne-Jones. *The Worcestershire Archive and Archaelology Services*

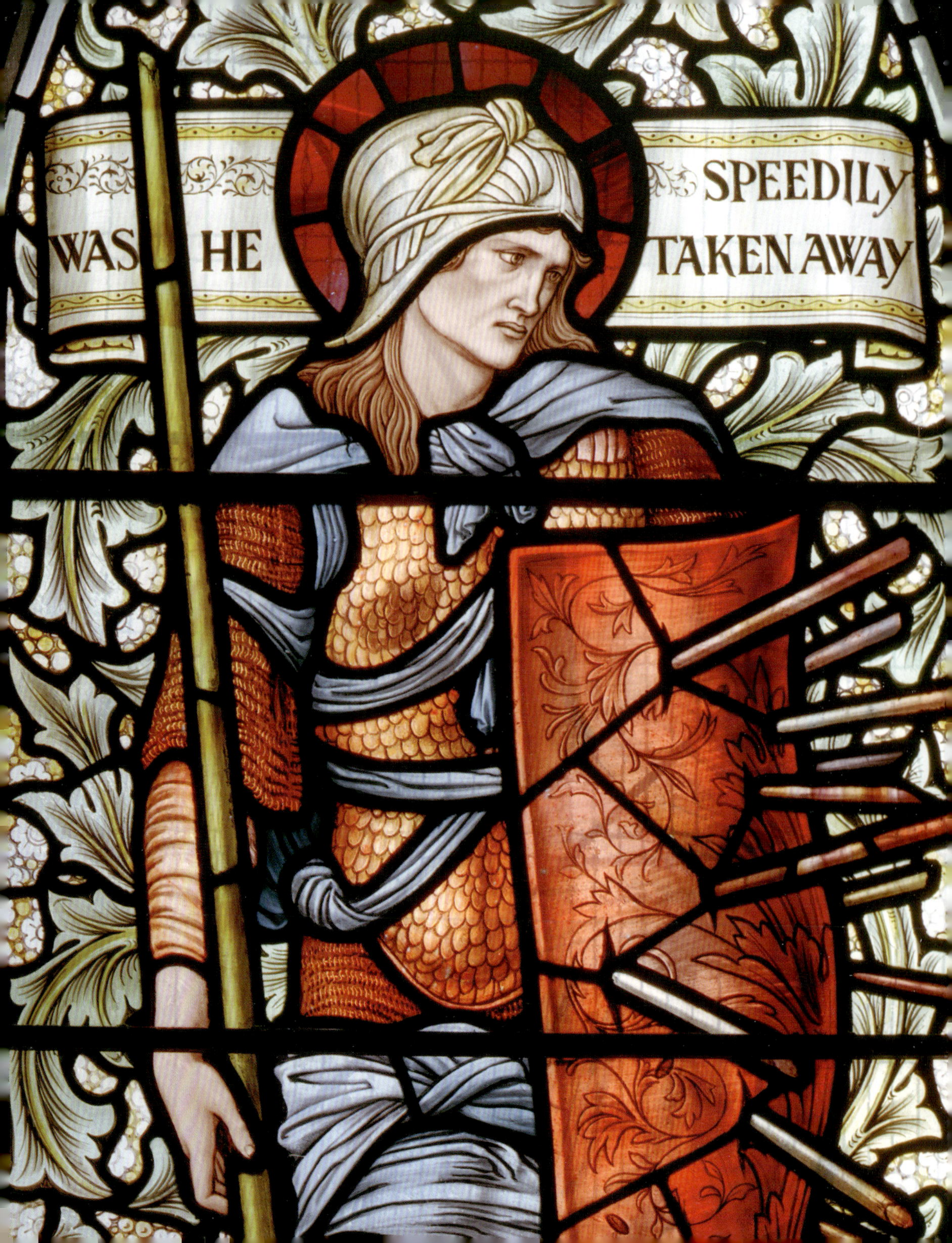
WAS HE
SPEEDILY
TAKEN AWAY

Fortitude and Triumph

Alfred's nephew is remembered in the window panels ***Fortitude*** and ***Triumph***. The accompanying inscription reads, ***To the Glory of God and in loving memory of Edward Arthur Baldwin who departed this life suddenly Jan 13. 1902 aged 37 Years.*** Edward Arthur had worked at the family's Stourport Iron Foundry and had become manager of the Anglo-American ***Tin Stamping Company***. He suffered a fatal heart attack while cycling between his home, The Mount (now better known as The Menzies Hotel, Stourport) and Wilden House. Outside in Wilden churchyard, his grave is shared by his wife Lucilla, who was also his first cousin; her epitaph names her as ***Lucilla Baldwin Baldwin***. Earlier tragedy struck the couple on the loss of their daughter Phyllis at eight months old. On this occasion they presented an illuminated prayer book to the church. The volume has an embroidered cover and gold tooled edges and may be seen on the altar on Open Days.

The window features two figures, ***Fortitude*** (BJ 229) and King Ethelbert or ***Triumph*** (BJ 534), and was placed in Wilden church on 15/06/1903. ***Fortitude*** was painted by Titcomb, and wears pink armour over which are wound blue drapes; she is protected by the long shield full of arrows. This device was first used by Morris & Co. in 1895 for a window in Horstead church, and a year later a slightly different version was installed in Meole Brace in which the figure wore a longer tunic and looked decidedly masculine, without hair showing below the helmet. A sketch supposedly drawn for St. Cuthbert's church, Newcastle, c.1896 is again a feminine version where the helmet is replaced by a halo, the skirt is modestly ankle-length and a lion adorns the shield. Burne-Jones explains in a client letter he *has doubts about Fortitude, but if her military symbols are left out she looks too like Patience.* Margaret Burne-Jones modelled for figures of both Prudence and Fortitude which were to be placed in St. Patrick's, Dublin, but the design was not installed. Frank Chadwick, whose factory provided workmen for Morris & Co., inherited the watercolour sketches when the Morris factory closed. A scroll behind the head bears the inscription ***Speedily was he taken away***. The wording continues into the adjacent window resuming in the scroll behind King Ethelbert's head; ***I opened not my mouth for it was thy doing***. These lines are from Psalm 39 and were included in the Order of Service for Burials.

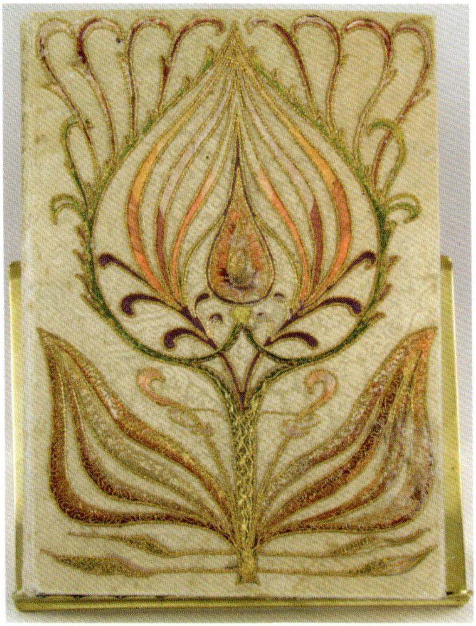

Triumph or King Ethelbert (BJ 534) was painted by Bowman, with foliage and scrolls drawn by Knight and painted by Wren. Ethelbert, King of

Left: Fortitude, detail.

Above: Illuminated Prayer Book presented by Lucilla and Edward Arthur Baldwin

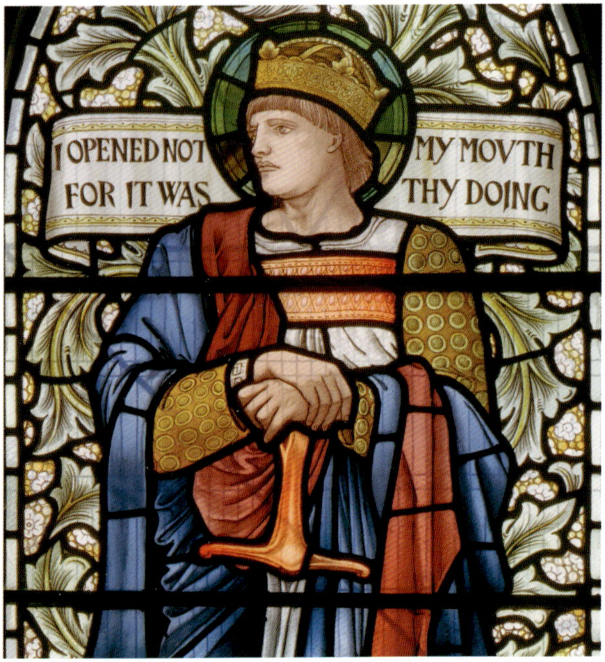

King Ethelbert, detail

Wessex, elder brother of Alfred the Great died in AD 866 and was buried in Sherborne. Burne-Jones produced two cartoons of the Saxon King and his wife for installation at Speldhurst. Here a churchwarden's notebook records that money had been submitted for Burne-Jones's cartoons, but not the glass. It was almost 20 years before the account was settled and the glass fitted. The two cartoons are now in the Birmingham Museum and Art Gallery, and the studio's sketch-design for the finished glass is in the William Morris Gallery in Walthamstow. The intricately detailed Wilden king wears a blue cloak lined with purple, his hands rest on his sword. The same figure appears in Malmesbury Abbey.

The Good Shepherd

The Good Shepherd or ***Love*** (BJ 339), in crimson, was painted by Stokes, with foliage background and ornamental base by Watson. This was the last window to be placed in the church on 06/10/1914 and has no dedication. The image of the Good Shepherd was popular among Pre-Raphaelite painters. Burne-Jones first produced a cartoon of this subject in 1857 whilst still working for James Powell & Son, after he was recommended by Dante Gabriel Rossetti. After viewing Burne-Jones's work, Rossetti wrote, *Christ is here represented as a real Shepherd, in such dress as is fit for walking the fields and hills. He carried lost sheep on his shoulder, and it is chewing some vine leaves which are wound round his hat - a lovely idea, is it not? A loaf and bottle of wine, the Sacred Elements, hang at His girdle; and behind Him is a wonderful piece of Gothic landscape.*

Later a more sophisticated cartoon was produced and used in 1880 for the first time in Brampton, Cumbria. The design has the reputation of being the most re-used of all Burne-Jones's stained glass designs. According to Sewter it has been used in at least 26 locations, other estimates suggest 44 different usages. Some were during Burne-Jones's lifetime while many were installed posthumously. At Wilden, as at most of these locations, the Christ figure is unusually represented as beardless, but at Whitfield and Brushford a beard has been added as in customary portrayals.

Right: The Good Shepherd, detail

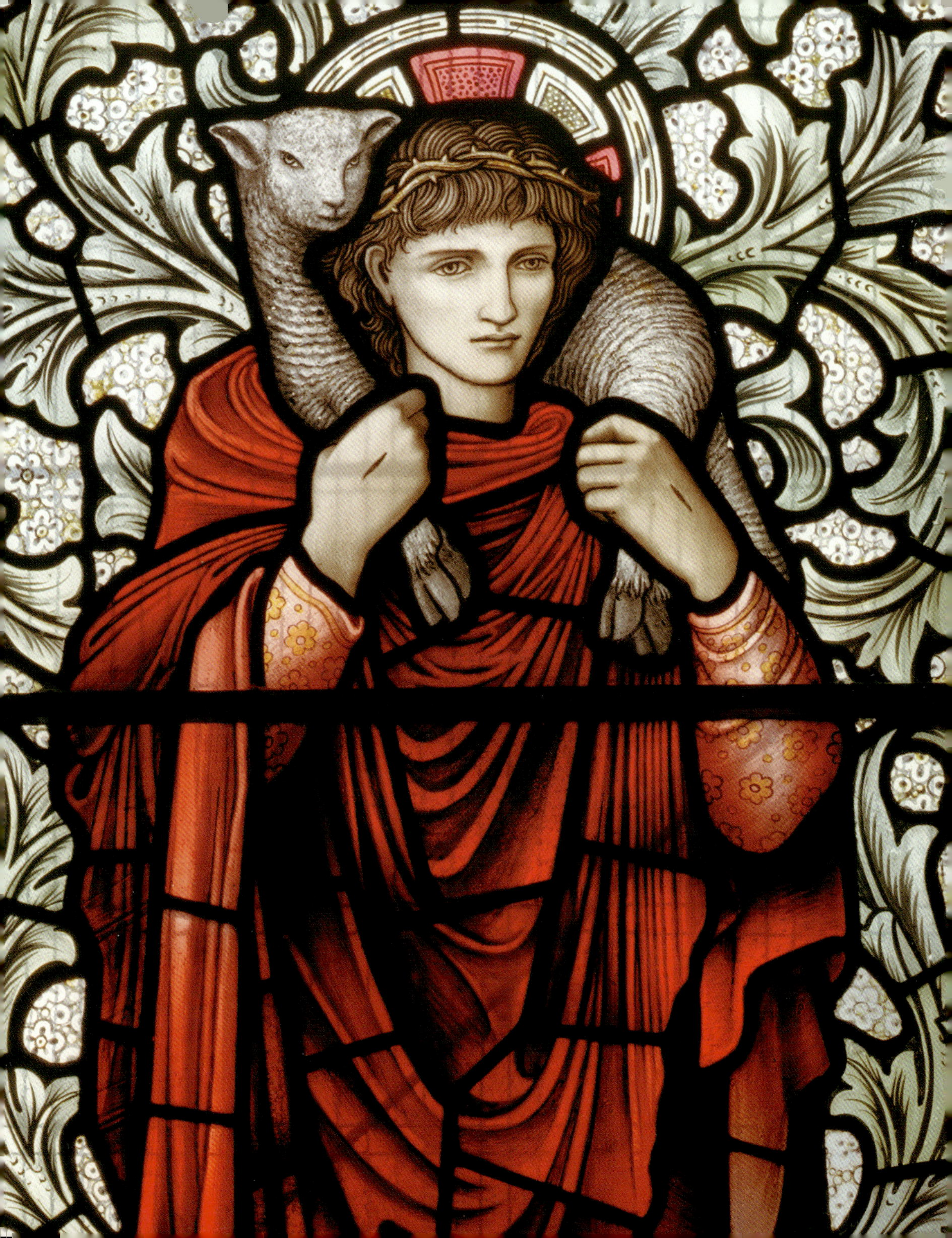

The West Windows

The Angels of Paradise (BJ, 411, 412, 413 & 414) of the west windows are recorded in Wilden's records on 29/08/1904. In the left window, the left light is by Bowman, the right light by Stokes, and the tracery angel by Titcomb, while the landscape, sky background and inscription were all by Wren. In the right window, the left light and the tracery angel are by Titcomb, the right light is by Stokes with the background and inscription painted by Wren. Many of Burne-Jones's female figures relate to music as can be seen here in these feminine instrument-carrying angels. The auburn-haired Pre-Raphaelite-style angels set against a glowing landscape conjure up a dreamlike vision of paradise. The angels wear flowing robes and on close inspection details of brocade work can be seen. They are not angels in pure white, but their gowns, wings and halos are in vivid shades of red, yellow and blue, yet they still stand out against the rich blues and greens of the background. The windows are particularly special when the sun is setting, filling them with additional radiance. These serene angels play harps, psalteries, hand organs and lutes as they descend and ascend paradise. In contrast the tracery angels hint at a different message, as like Joshua's army, they blow strident trumpets.

Alfred Baldwin was again responsible for funding the windows placed as memorials to important figures and friends. Under the left window, left panel, the inscription reads ***To the Glory of God and in Memory of Dr Henry Philpott sometime Bishop of Worcester and of John Haviland sometime Rector of Hartlebury***.

Henry Philpott, born in1807 was elected Vice-Chancellor to the University of Cambridge on three occasions. In 1847 he was awarded the degree of Doctor of Divinity. Philpott was Bishop of Worcester from 1860-1890, and was instrumental in founding All Saints, Wilden, guiding Alfred through the intricacies of changing parish boundaries. He played a major role in the consecration service of 1880. John Haviland, Rector of Hartlebury was also present at this first service, as Wilden came under his pastoral care as a Chapel of Ease. All Saints became a parish in its own right in 1904, when then curate, William J. Cory was promoted to being Wilden's first vicar.

Under the left window, right panel, the inscription is, ***To the Glory of God in grateful memory of William John Butler, sometime Vicar of Wantage.*** William Butler was appointed as Vicar of Wantage in1846. In 1880 he became Canon of Worcester, and presumably this is when he became acquainted with Alfred Baldwin. In 1885 he was appointed Dean of Lincoln. Arthur John Butler wrote ***Life and letters of William John Butler: late Dean of Lincoln and sometime Vicar of Wantage: with portraits.*** The book includes in its title the same intriguing description of William Butler as *sometime* Vicar of Wantage. The word *sometime* appears three times in these two memorial lines, whether as space filler or an intentional word that would be chargeable. The inscription relating to the right window reads across both panels; ***To the Glory of God and in loving memory of Three***

Right: The west windows

Overleaf: Details of Angels of Paradise from the west windows

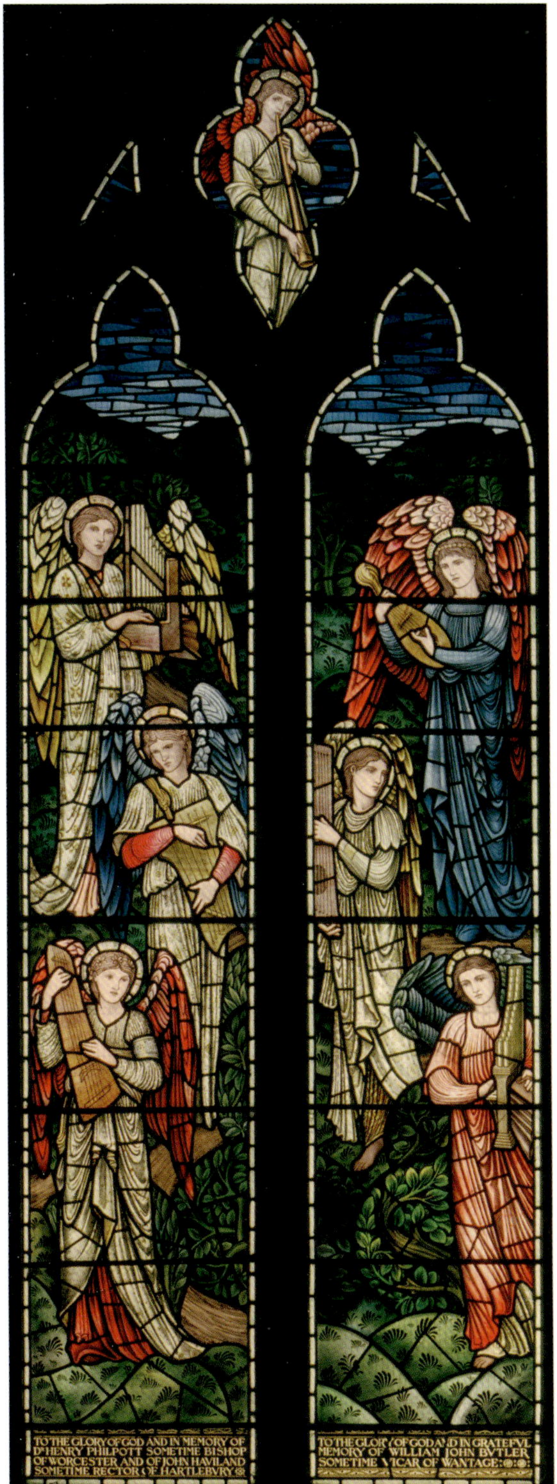
TO THE GLORY OF GOD AND IN MEMORY OF
Dr HENRY PHILPOTT SOMETIME BISHOP
OF WORCESTER AND OF JOHN HAVILAND
SOMETIME RECTOR OF HARTLEBVRY
TO THE GLORY OF GOD AND IN GRATEFVL
MEMORY OF WILLIAM JOHN BVTLER
SOMETIME VICAR OF WANTAGE

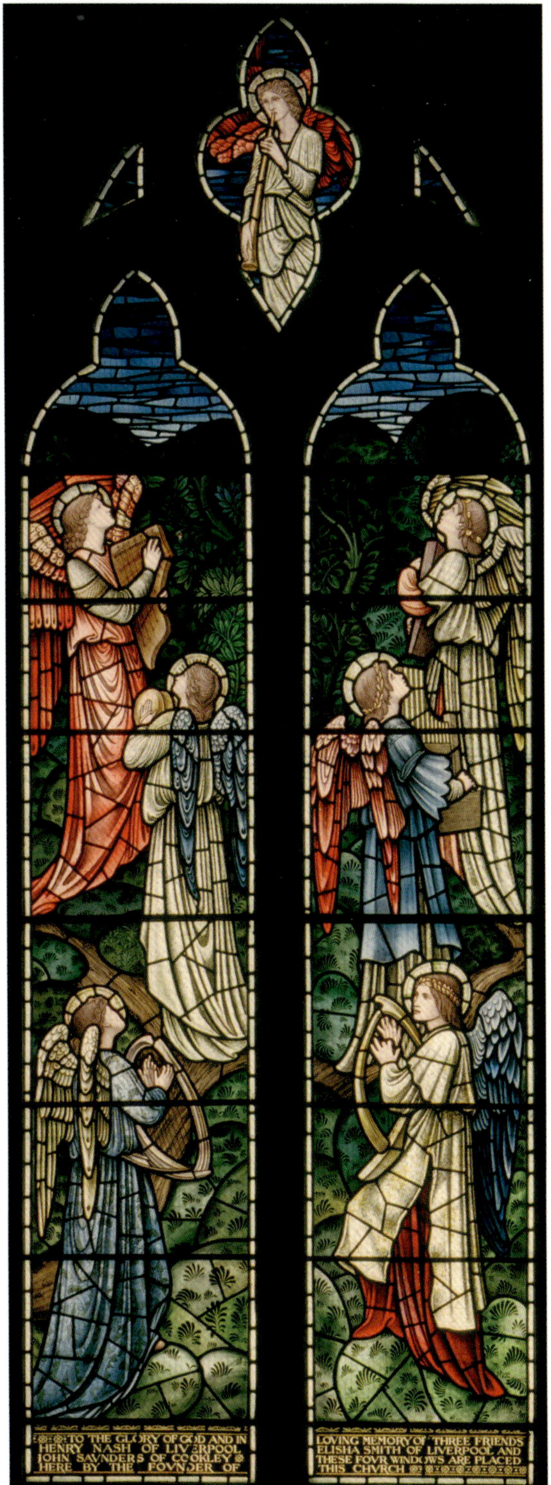
TO THE GLORY OF GOD AND IN
HENRY NASH OF LIVERPOOL
JOHN SAVNDERS OF COOKLEY
HERE BY THE FOVNDER OF
LOVING MEMORY OF THREE FRIENDS
ELISHA SMITH OF LIVERPOOL AND
THESE FOVR WINDOWS ARE PLACED
THIS CHVRCH

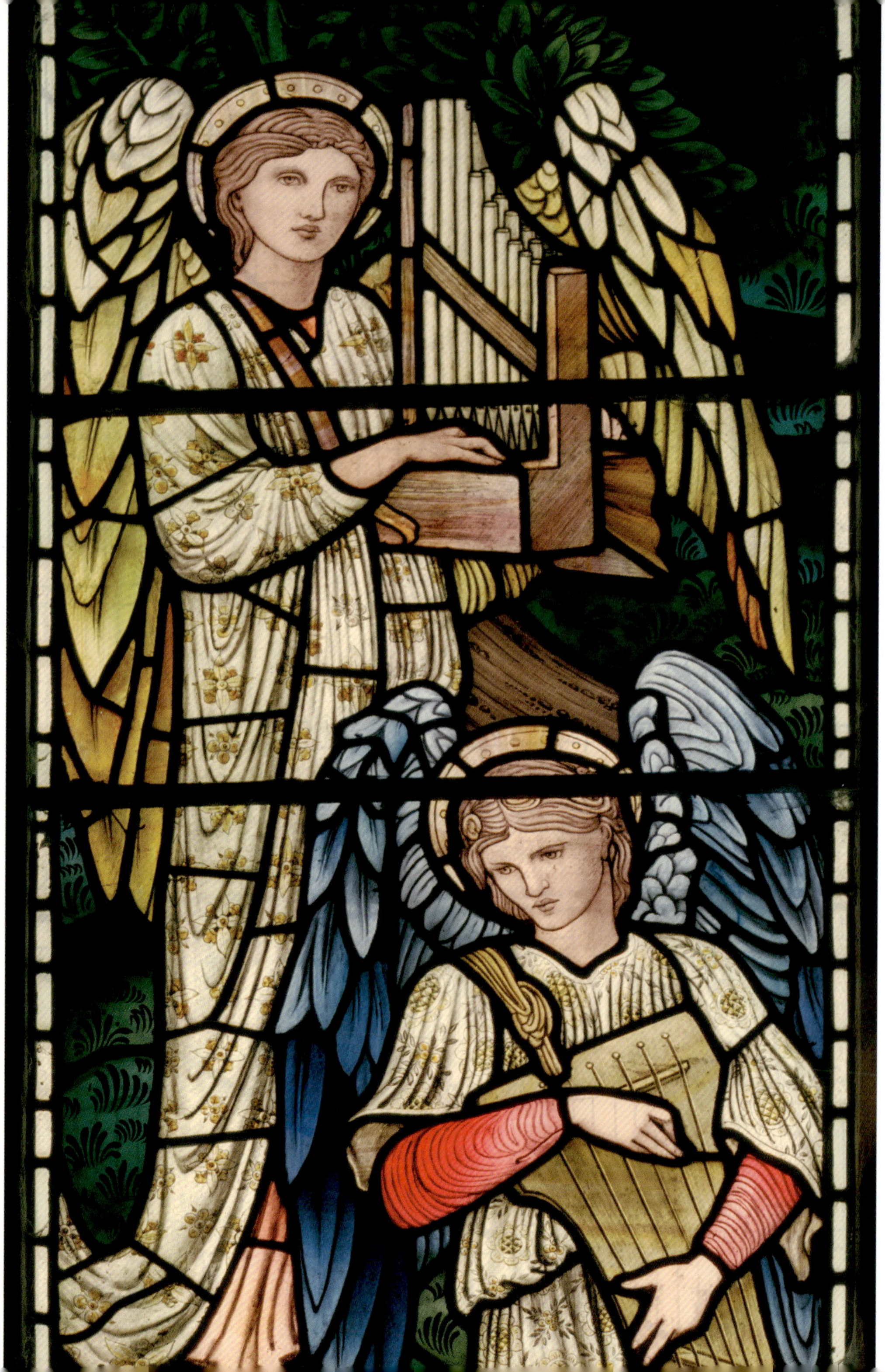

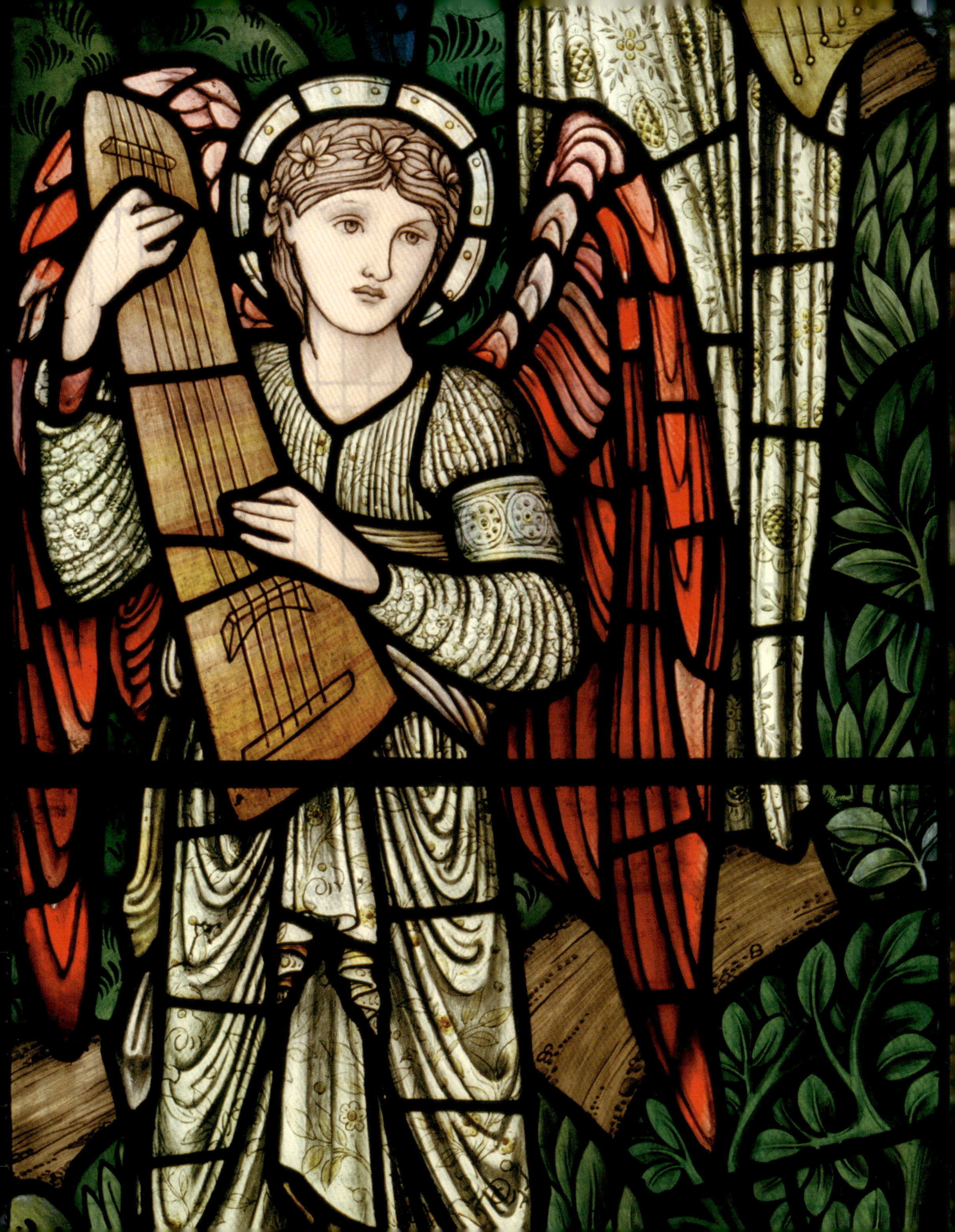

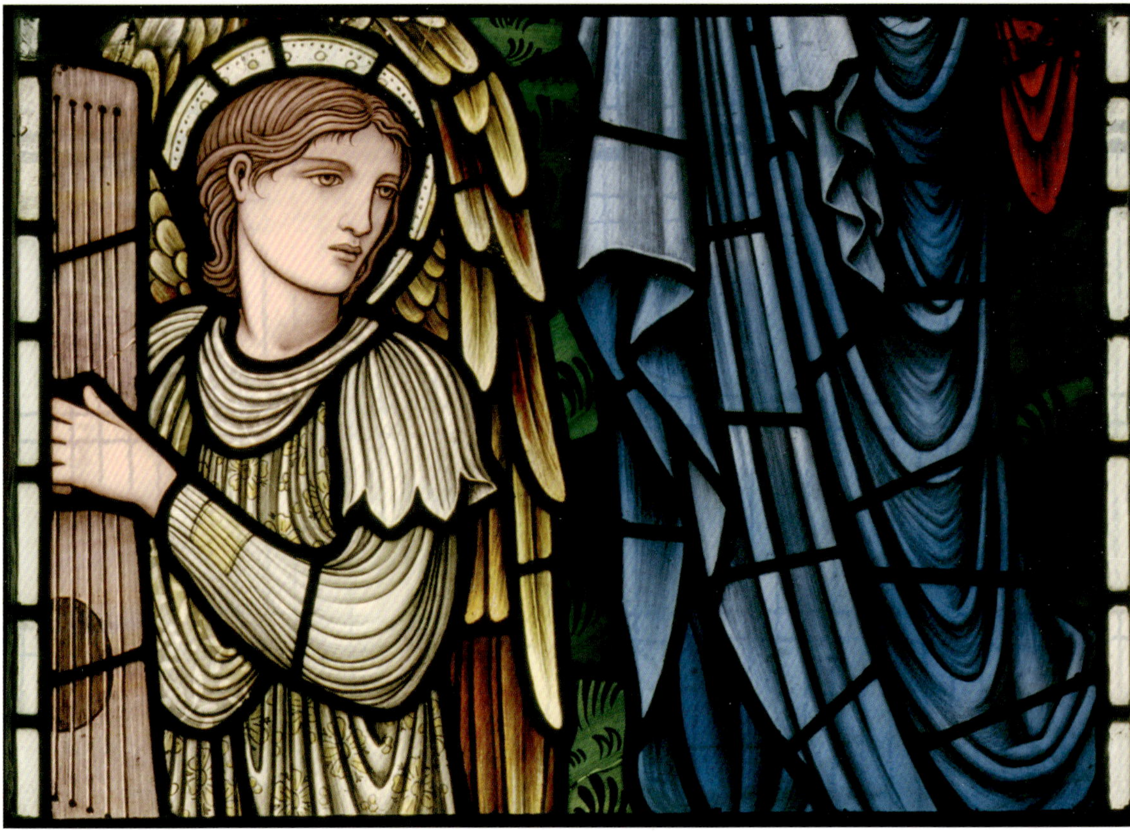

Above and *Right:* Angels of Paradise, west window details

Friends Henry Nash of Liverpool, Elisha Smith of Liverpool and John Saunders of Cookley. These four windows are placed here by the founder of this church. Less is known of these friends who did not seem to have important *sometime* positions. John Saunders, Ironmaster is listed in Cookley's Parish records as living in Wolverley Cottage, Cookley.

The Angels of Paradise were designed in 1881 for All Hallows, Allerton. Since then either or both windows have been installed in the church of the Incarnation, New York in 1885; Westminster, St. Stephen, 1890; Leigh, 1890; Nutfield, 1892; Wilden, 1904 and Carnoustie, 1906.

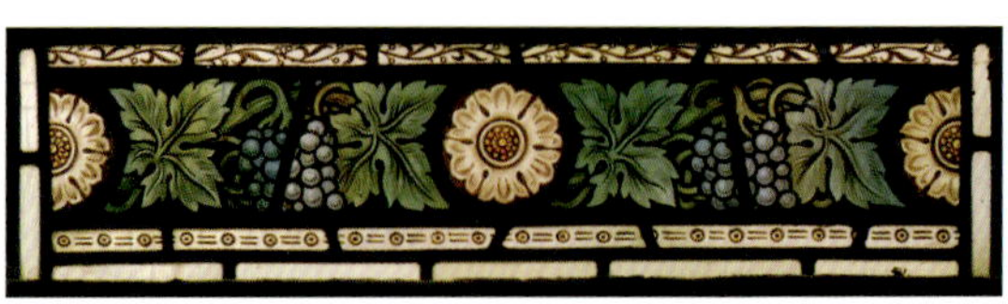

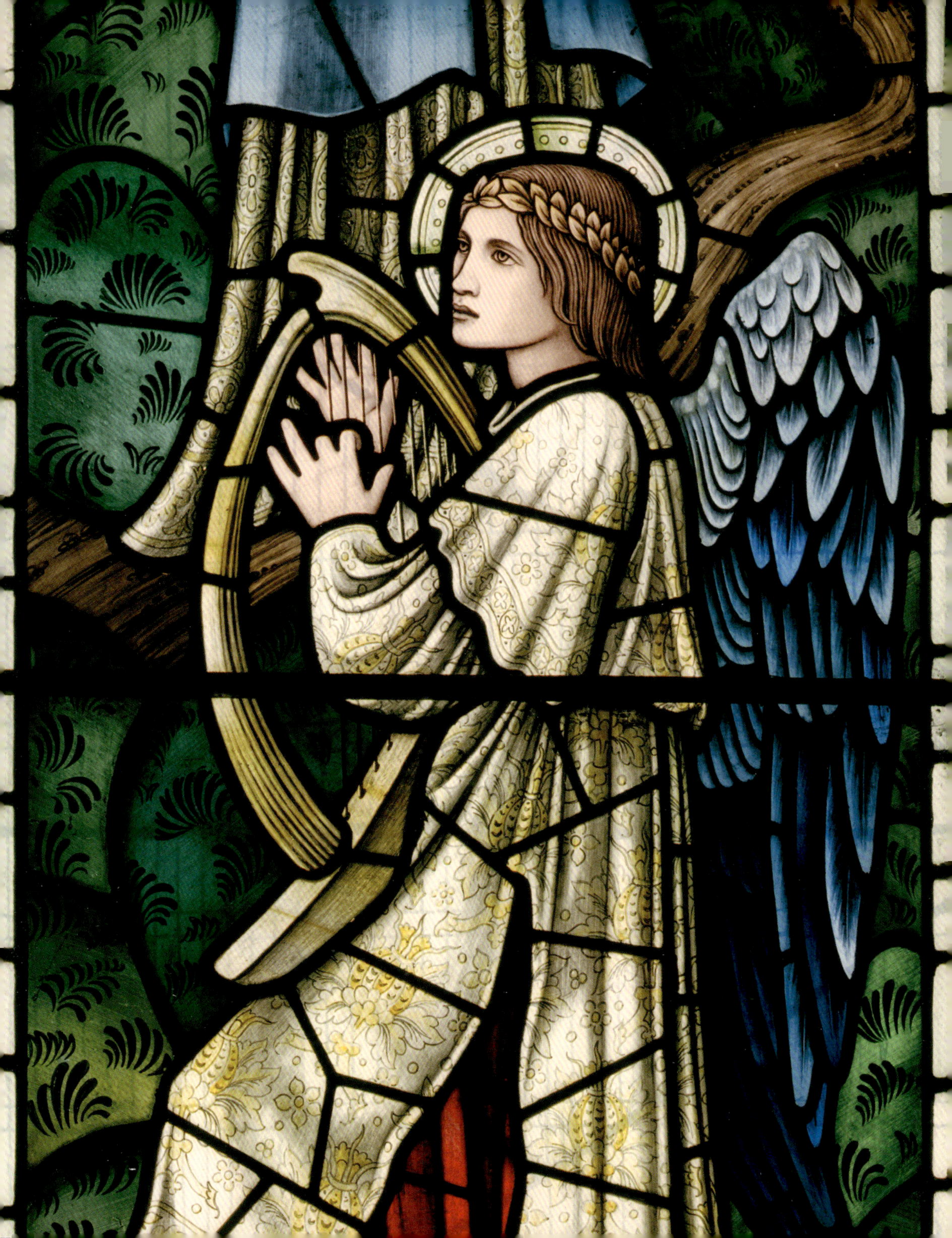

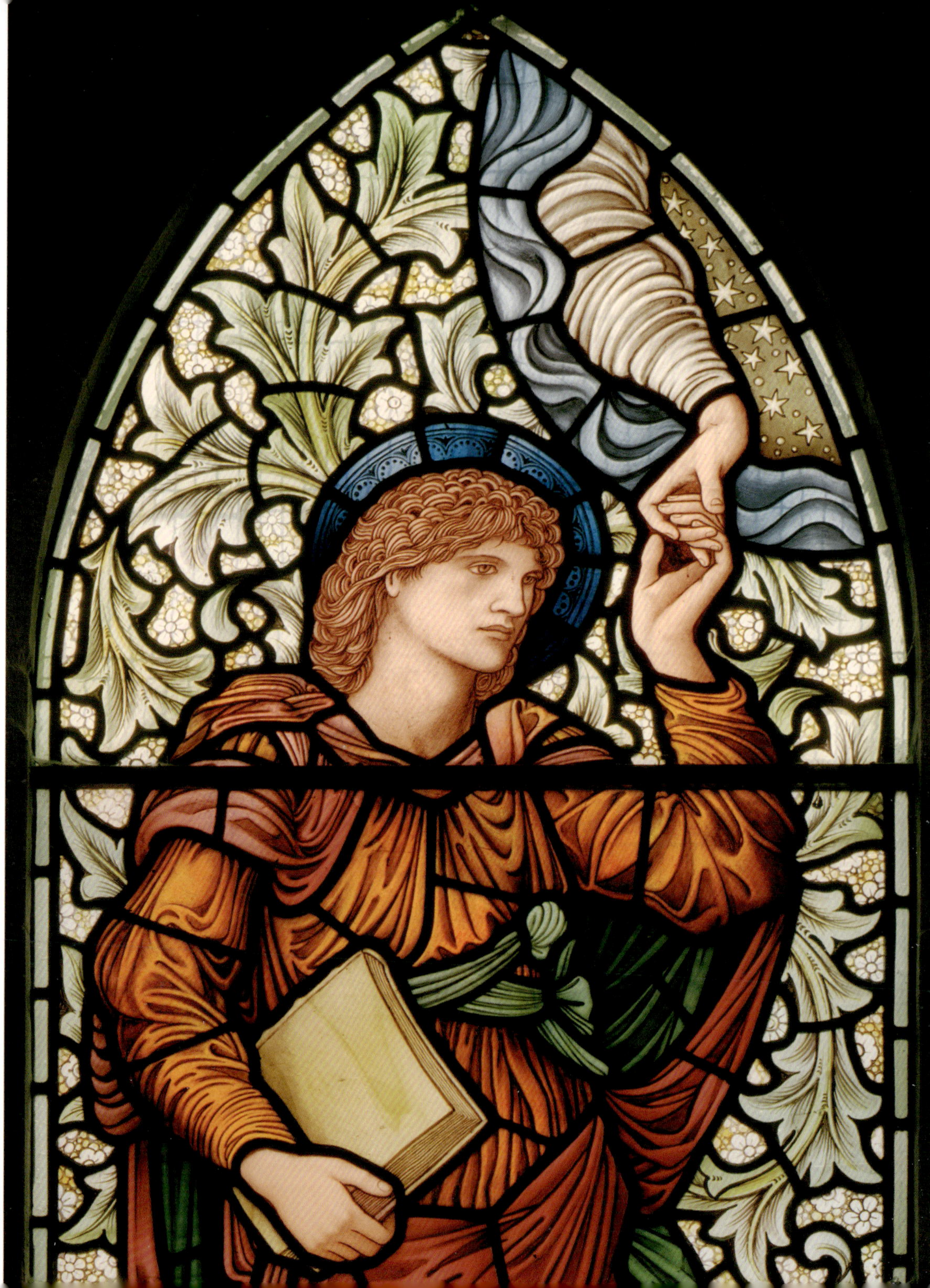

The Enoch Window

Enoch (BJ 143) was placed in Wilden on 05/07/1907 and painted by Stokes. Burne-Jones originally designed this figure of the Old Testament prophet for the west window of Calcutta Cathedral in 1874. It was adapted by Morris & Co. for windows in 26 other locations, including those at St. Martin's, Brampton; Holy Trinity, Sloane Street, Chelsea; Leigh, Cullompton Devon; Harris Manchester College, Oxford; Holy Trinity, Meole Brace and Cheadle Hospital Chapel.

The inscription reads ***In memory of Enoch Baldwin who departed this life June 11, 1905 aged 82 years.*** Enoch Baldwin was brother to George Pearce Baldwin. He was Alfred Baldwin's uncle, and a member of the family firm of ***Baldwin, Son & Co.*** In 1880, Baldwin was elected Member of Parliament for Bewdley and held the seat until 1885. He subsequently became JP for Worcestershire and in March 1889 a County Councillor. Baldwin lived at The Mount, Stourport and died at the age of 82. The biblical Enoch was a descendant of Adam, son of Jared, father to Methuselah and ancestor of Jesus. *Enoch lived in fellowship with God for 300 years and had other children. He lived to be 365 years old and then he disappeared because God took him away* (Gen.5: 22-24). Enoch is depicted grasping the Hand of God which reaches from the starry heavens from behind the rolled-back sky. This appears to signify the death of Enoch; the prophet Elijah was carried up to heaven in a fiery chariot, but Enoch simply *walked with God.*

The Felton Window

The double window in the north wall of the nave was installed on 15/11/1900 and features ***Timothy*** (BJ 23) and ***Samuel*** (BJ 22). A cryptic note in the church record also states *headed Mrs Baldwin's 'W'.* ***Samuel*** (BJ 22) in crimson was painted by Stokes. In the book of Samuel this prophet and last Judge of the Israelites was awoken from sleep when he heard his name called. Twice he assumed Eli called him, but after the second time Eli realized it was God calling Samuel. He told him *Go back to bed; and if he calls you again, say, Speak Lord, your servant is listening.* In a scroll behind Samuel's head is written, ***Loquere Domine quia audit servus tuus;*** Eli's instruction in Latin.

Timothy (BJ 23), wearing dark green and blue, was painted by Bowman with background foliage drawn by Knight and painted by Wren. The inscription is also by Wren. Samuel and Timothy are clad in calf-length, open-toed legwear; these garments seem impractical but give full scope for drawing artistic folds. Burne-Jones produced the Timothy cartoon in 1872 for a window in Christ Church Cathedral, Oxford. His account book records a charge of £12 for *Big Timothy* in contrast to a smaller design of Timothy and Eunice for the same Oxford window. The design was used for a number of windows in schools, including: William Morris's own school, Marlborough College in 1877, Forest School, Walthamstow, 1881, where Morris's brothers had been pupils and Cheadle Hospital Chapel. Timothy, son of a Jewish mother and a Gentile father, was travelling companion to St. Paul. His mother, Eunice, and grandmother, Lois, were believers in Jesus and Timothy had great knowledge of scriptures, and was co-author of seven of Paul's epistles. In the scroll behind Timothy's head is a Latin phrase *Dabit tibi dominus in omnibus intellectu*, taken from 2 Timothy 2:7,

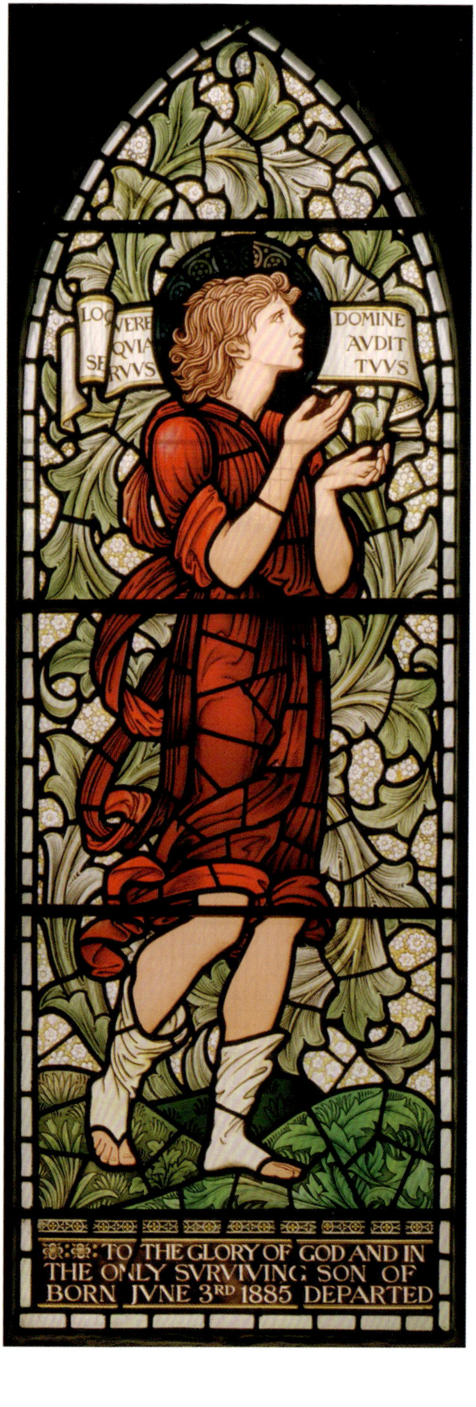

being the second part of the verse, translating as *Understand what I am saying. For the Lord will give you understanding in all things.*

The double window was dedicated to ***William Felton, only surviving son of William and Phoebe Felton***. William Felton was on the management Committee at Wilden Works. He and his wife had lost one son in infancy, but when William died aged 15 they were inconsolable. There is no mention in church of their seven surviving daughters; the youngest of whom was named Septima, as suggested by Louisa Baldwin. One of the daughters married a worker from the factory, and although the Ironworks operated as a family concern with Alfred knowing employees by name, there were still hierarchical social levels, and this marriage did not earn approval. Another daughter made a more acceptable choice, marrying William Henry Cory, Curate at Wilden who then became its first Vicar in 1904. The links between Wilden Ironworks and church existed in matters commonplace or spiritual.

Left: Samuel

Right: Timothy, detail

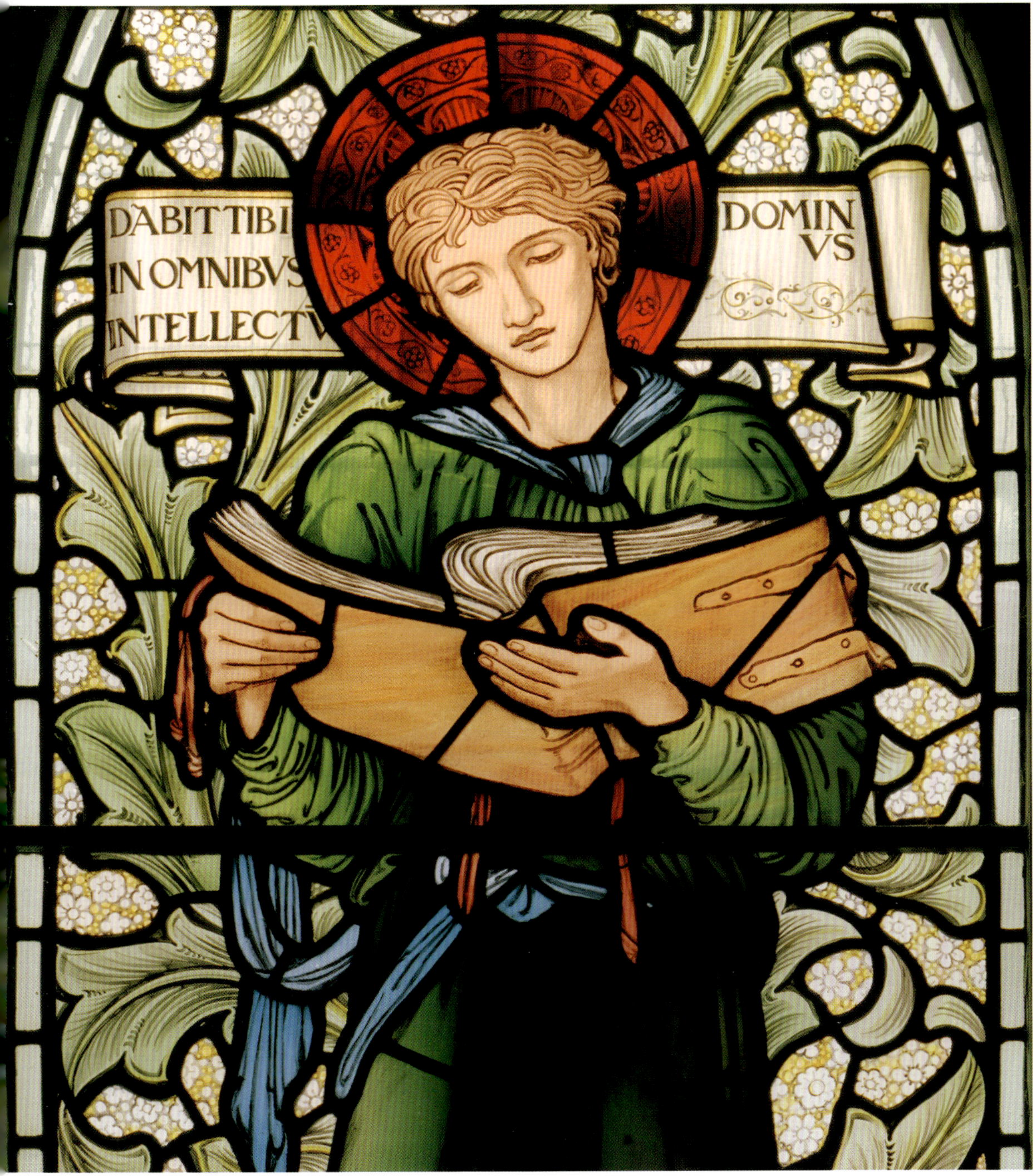
DABIT TIBI
IN OMNIBVS
INTELLECTV
DOMIN
VS

The St. Agnes Window

St. Agnes or ***Humility*** (BJ 335) was installed in Wilden on 05/07/1907, the year following the death of Agnes (MacDonald) Poynter. The window fittingly depicts St. Agnes holding a lamb and was painted by Titcomb, with background foliage drawn by Knight and painted by Wren. The inscription is also by Wren, and reads: ***In memory of Agnes Poynter who put on immortality June 1906. Dedicated by her sister Louisa Baldwin***. Agnes was regarded as the family beauty. Said to have the most *symmetrical* face she had modelled in her youth for Burne-Jones. Agnes played the piano and sang, and was said to be the most musical of the MacDonald sisters. It was love of music which first drew Agnes and Edward Poynter together. This design also appears in Macclesfield, Cheshire, Walton, Liverpool and St Giles, Edinburgh, in each case depicting St. Agnes who was martyred in Rome in the 4th Century.

Other Treasures

Other treasures at Wilden include the silver communion plate, or paten, given to the church by Alfred's wife, Louisa along with a silver chalice and a wine ewer. The vessels are based on Bishop Fox's Plate at Corpus Christi College, Oxford of 1508. They are all inscribed ***The gift of L.B. to All Saints, Wilden, All Saints Day 1895***, hallmarked London 1895, and set with Louisa's personal jewels. One of the couple's grandsons was later to describe how on their honeymoon in Scotland, Alfred bought Louisa a tartan shawl and a *Scottish silver brooch* with which to fasten it. It is believed that this is the thistle-shaped amethyst brooch set in the wine jug. The vessels are displayed in church on festival days.

The church possesses a set of Arts and Crafts *Flying Angel* drapes which replicate the angels of the glorious east windows. An altar frontispiece intricately worked in gold thread is based on a William Morris *vine and grapes* design. Worked mainly by Edith MacDonald, after taking several years to complete, the frontispiece was first used on Easter Sunday 1891. Edith did not marry and lived with her mother, after whose death she came to live in Wilden House. Louisa suffered poor health, and spent much time confined to bed. Edith was then on hand to help with Stanley's upbringing. She was the last resident of Wilden House; after her death in 1939 Wilden House was demolished as part of a road widening scheme.

The Organ

From the laying of the foundation stone of the church in 1879, it was clear that music would be important in All Saints. Louisa and her sisters had excellent singing voices and were proficient instrumentalists and it is believed that Alfred wished to employ the finest organ builders of the day. Rival firms Hill and Willis were asked to tender for the job of providing an instrument to enrich worship. ***Henry Willis & Sons*** gained the contract. From 1847 *Father Willis* had

Right: St. Agnes, detail

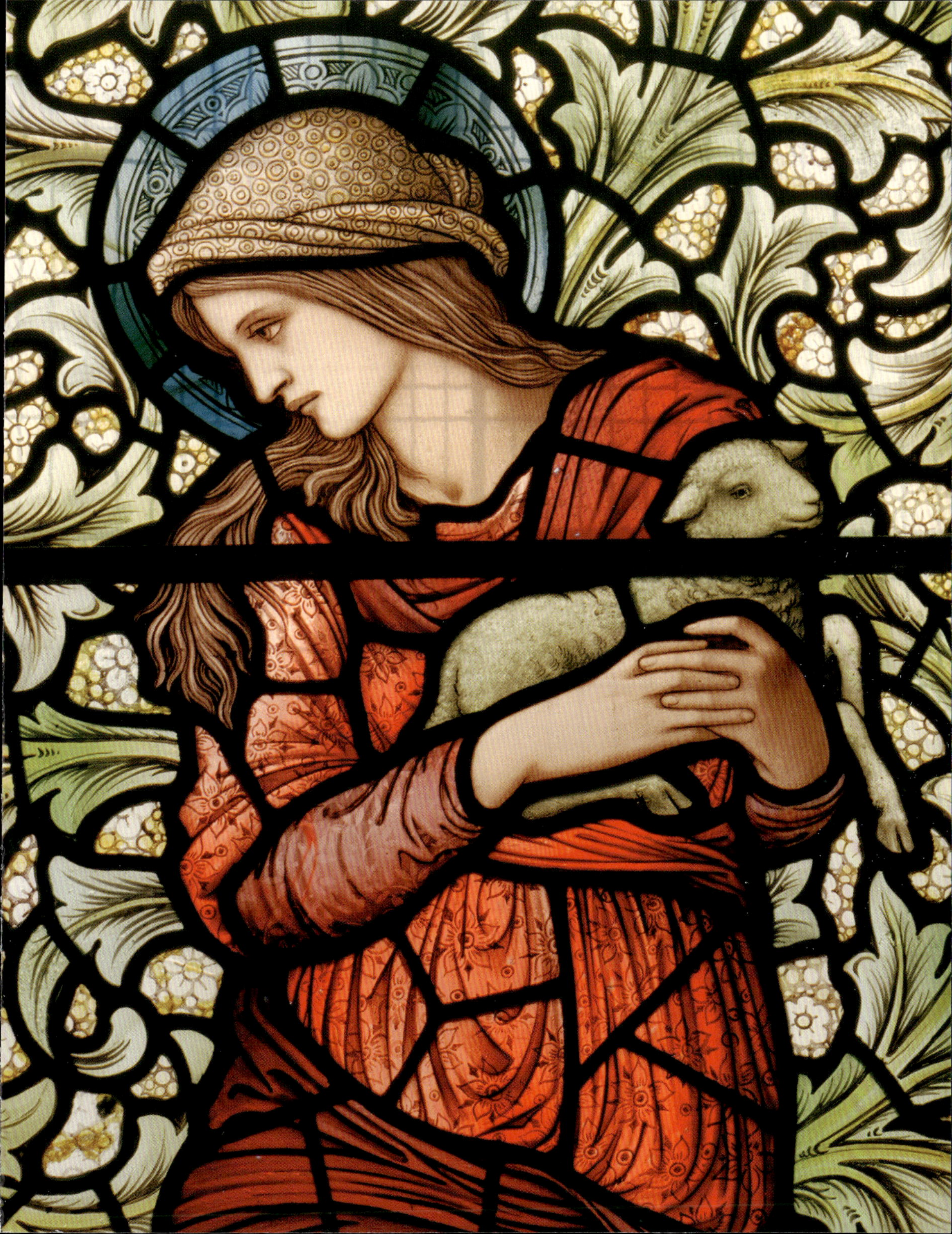

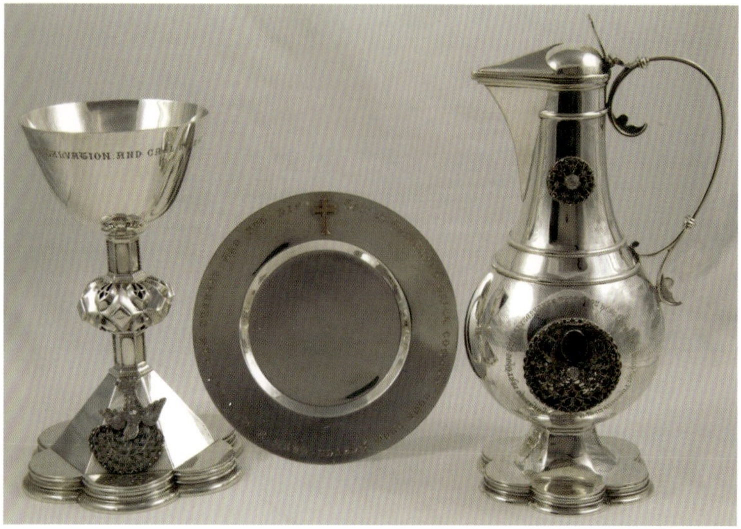

specialised in building great organs for British cathedrals, including St. Pauls, London. He had learnt to play the organ at an early age, becoming organist of Christ Church, Hoxton as a teenager. A life-changing opportunity came when he moved to Cheltenham, to work with instrument-maker W.E. Evans and met Samuel Sebastian Wesley. Through Wesley, Henry was offered the contract to rebuild the organ of Gloucester Cathedral. He commented, *I received £400 for the job, and I was presumptuous enough to marry.*

Later, with a family Henry set up business with his sons Henry Willis II and Henry Willis III constructing instruments in *The Rotunda Organ Works* Rochester Place, London. It was here the Wilden organ came into being. This was a time of craft industry. Great pride was taken in every instrument built to Willis's exacting standards, benefitting from his skill in pipe voicing. The construction of the Wilden Willis Organ was typical of Victorian engineering at that time. The moving components and structural elements, though hidden from view, were built with care and a sense of beauty and form. The organ was placed in the church in 1880, the first organist being F.A. Griffiths. Stanley Baldwin was encouraged to follow the musical traditions of his mother's side of the family. In 1885 his father's diary entry states *I have just had a good walk with Stan across the Common, and now he is gone to have an organ lesson from Griffiths.*

The Baldwin Legacy

Regular services and Open Days ensure that the church shares its treasures and visitors are able to witness the legacy left by a caring businessman and his artistic relatives. Wilden's windows are a testament to an industrialist who was prepared to fight the fight of faith, *put on the gospel armour* and lead by example. The windows installed by this benefactor fill the church with the light of inspiration and truly call for *praising the Lord in song with instruments.*

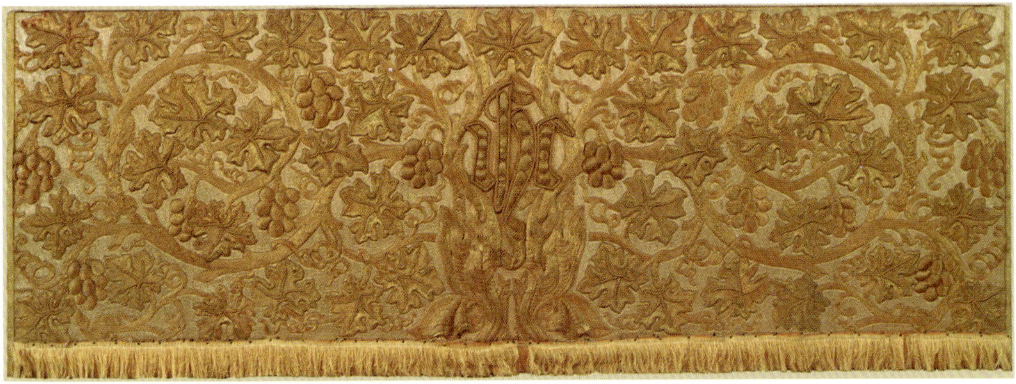

Left: Silver Chalice, Paten and Wine Ewer set with Louisa Baldwin's personal jewels

Above: Alter Frontispiece embroidered by Edith MacDonald

Below: Arts and Crafts Angel Drape, detail

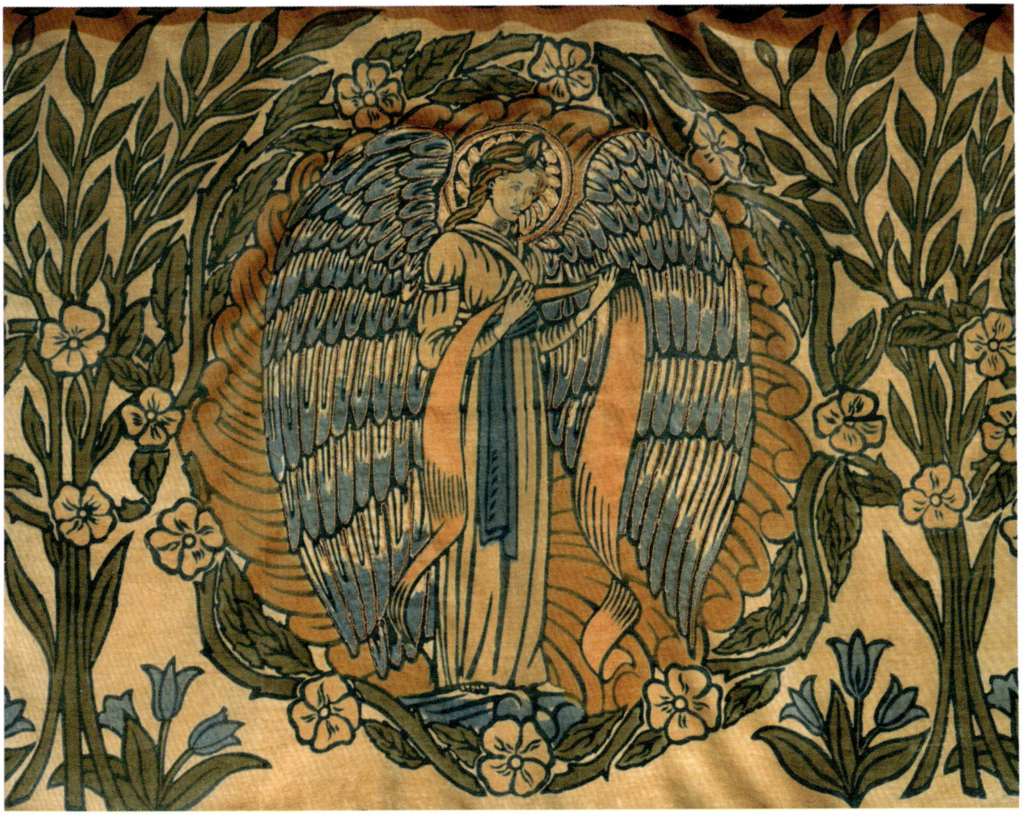

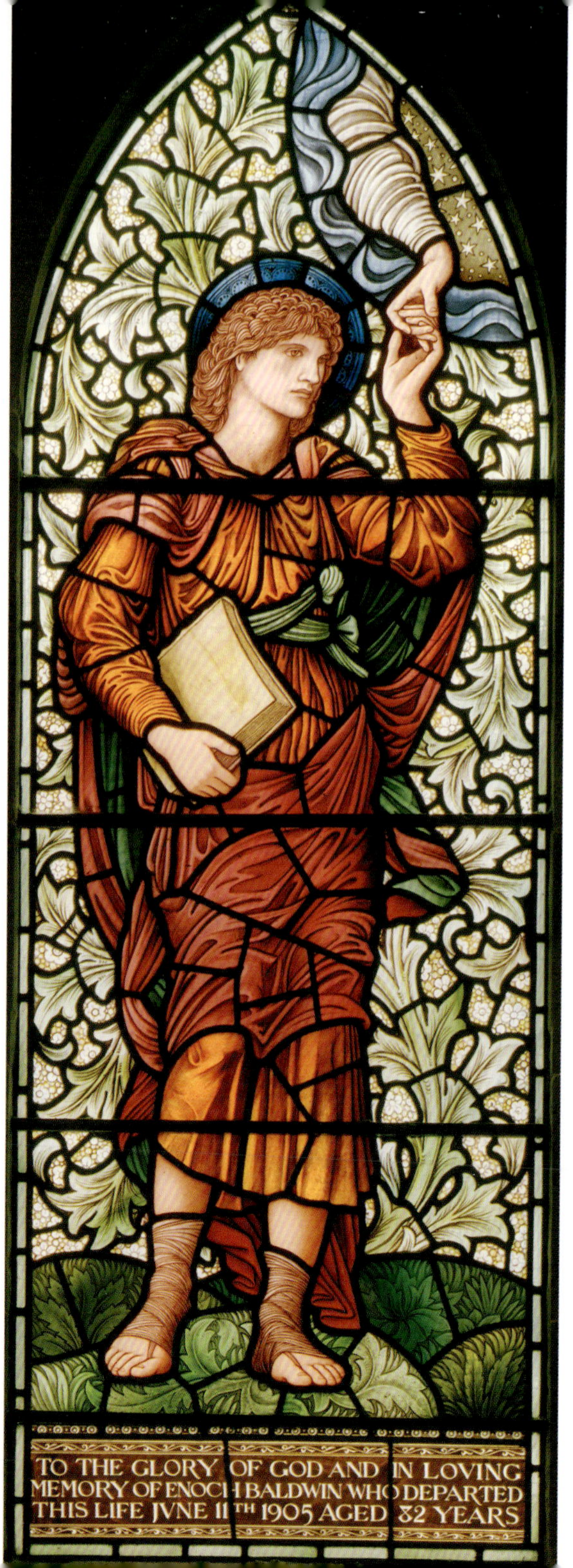
TO THE GLORY OF GOD AND IN LOVING
MEMORY OF ENOCH BALDWIN WHO DEPARTED
THIS LIFE JVNE 11TH 1905 AGED 32 YEARS

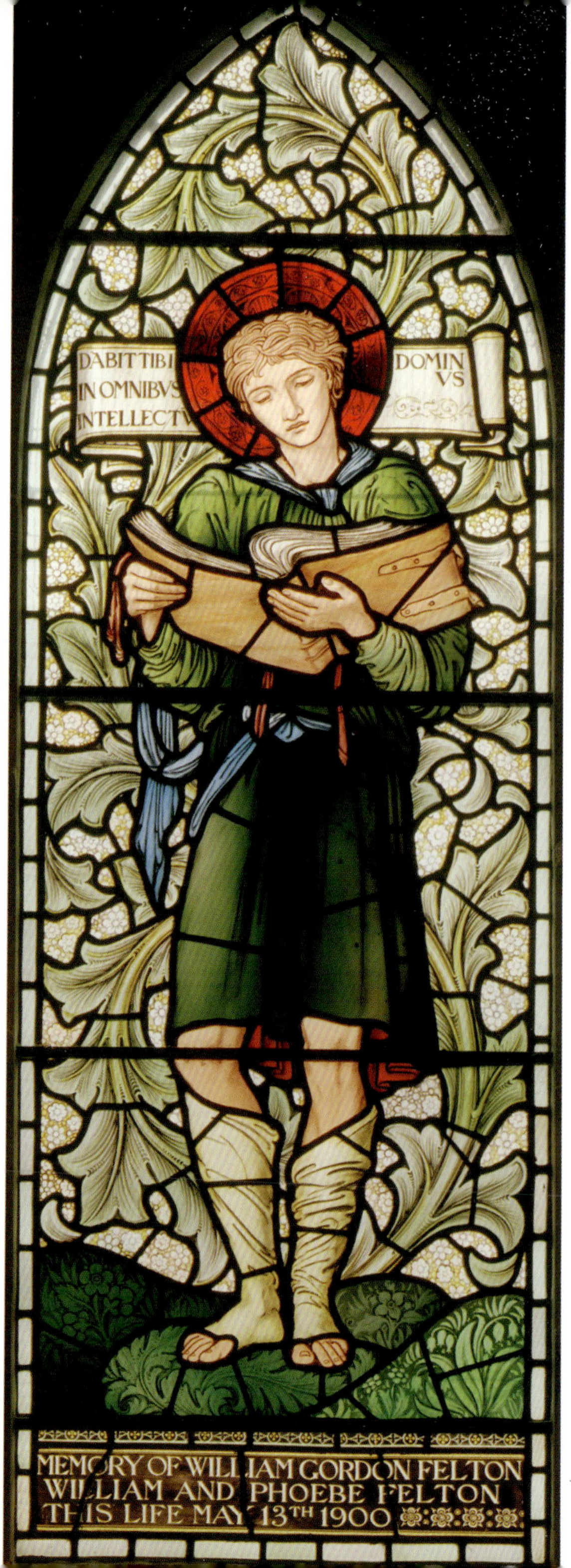
DABITTIBI
IN OMNIBVS
INTELLECTV
DOMIN
VS
MEMORY OF WILLIAM GORDON FELTON
WILLIAM AND PHOEBE FELTON
THIS LIFE MAY 13TH 1900

Bibliography

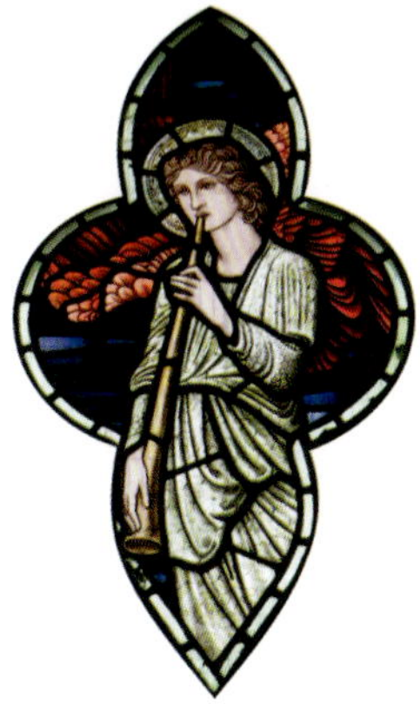

All Saints Wilden, church records, inventories and log book.

Correspondence between Earl Baldwin, Wilden PCC and Lowndes & Drury, Worcestershire Archive and Archaeology Service.

The Bible. English New International Version.

Annis, P. 2010. *Searching for Monica Baldwin*. Stourport Civic Society.

Baldwin, A.W. 1955. *My Father: The True Story*. George Allen & Unwin Ltd, London.

Malcolm Bell. 1892. *Sir Edward Burne-Jones; a record and review*. George Bell & Son, London and New York.

Benyon, T. 2011. Stained glass workers employed by James Powell & Sons and by Morris, Marshall, Faulkner & Company and Morris & Company: a biographical listing. In *The Journal of Stained Glass, Volume XXXV*, pp.242-56.

Barringer, T. 1998. *The Pre-Raphaelites: Reading the Image*. The Everyman Library, Calmann & King, London.

Cormack, P. 2008. *Morris & Company's Stained glass For The Chapel of Cheadle Royal Hospital*. Haslam & Whiteway Ltd.

Craven, P. 2006. *All Saints Parish, Wilden: a hidden treasure.*

The Family & Local History Handbook 10. Robert Blatchford Publishing Ltd, York. pp.213-215.

Flanders, J. 2001. *A Circle of Sisters; Alice Kipling, Georgiana Burne-Jones, Agnes Poynter and Louisa Baldwin*. Viking, London.

Pevsner, N. 1968. *The Buildings of England: Worcestershire*. Harmondsworth: Penguin Books.

Schoenherr, Douglas E. 2005. The Cartoon Book and Morris & Company's sale of Burne-Jones's cartoons in 1901-1904. *The Journal of Stained Glass, Volume XXIX.*

Sewter. A.C. 1974, 1975. *The Stained Glass of William Morris and his Circle*, published in two volumes by Yale University Press, New Haven and London.

Shenton, Kenneth. 2001. *A great Victorian Henry Willis 1821–1901*. The Organist's Review.

Far Left: Enoch

Left: Timothy

Above and *Overleaf:* West window tracery, Angels

Inside back cover: Left, The Good Shepherd, *Right:* St. Agnes

Back cover: East window tracery, Angel with Dulcimer

Acknowledgements

The Authors would like to thank the following for all their support and encouragement:

Andrea Miller, Richard Cory, Wilden PCC, Ray Franks, William Waters.

Worcestershire Archive and Archaeology Service 850WILDEN/9410/6/1/1-70

Many thanks to Steve Jones of Palm Laboratories Ltd for all his hard work with processing and scanning beyond the call of duty. www.palmlabs.co.uk

Printed by John Price Printers Ltd, Brook Street, Bilston, WV14 0NW.
Typeset in Adobe Caslon Pro.

ISBN 978-0-9532801-4-8

Designed and Published by Seraphim Press Ltd
Home Farm, Abbots Morton, Worcs WR7 4NA
www.alastaircarew-cox.com

All Saints, Wilden Lane, Wilden, Worcestershire, DY13 9LP
Tel: 01299 878224

pamela.craven@btopenworld.com

The Pre-Raphaelite Society www.pre-raphaelitesociety.org email : info@pre-raphaelitesociety.org

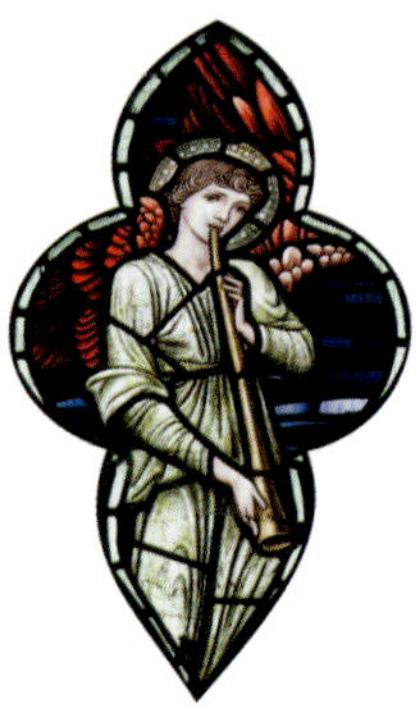